The Thinking Log

the Thinking LOG

a novel

R. RACHEL GAUNA

Never stop loving!

R. Rachel Gauna

it's about love
♥ publishing for a cause

it's about love
P.O. Box 51264
Amarillo, TX 79159-1264
www.pub4cause.com
+1.858.449.0706

Edited by Sally Arteseros
Proofread by by Katie Herman
Author photo: JJ Huckin
Book design by TLC Graphics, *www.TLCGraphics.com*
Cover design: Tamara Dever
Interior design: Erin Stark

Cover image © www.123rf.com/profile_maryvoo

ISBN: 978-0-9987170-0-5
Library of Congress Control Number: 2017906299

Printed in the United States of America by Cenveo Trafton

First American Edition

Dedicated to all the peeps out there
who walk the streets of kindness
with big juicy hearts.
Peace.

Kind words are a honeycomb,
Sweet to the soul and healing to the bones.

PROVERBS 16:24

prologue

THE GROVE OF TREES FORMS silhouettes against a cloudless, reddish-orange backdrop. The spring evening air is cool on my face. It is quiet. I can hear everything. The sounds are of rustling leaves as whatever random deer or rabbit scurries to its next point in nature. A wolf's howl echoes in the distance. The gush of water from the nearby creek continues its flow. Tears are flowing down my cheeks, as I reach deep into my mind, for the sound of a time before, as a child with my parents, wishing they were here with me, even if just one more time. To hear their voices right now, in real life, and not recorded by memory, would be perfect.

If you had asked me a year ago where I might see myself today, my prediction would not have been this. Not even close. My response would have included wedding bells ringing in a new season, with celebratory tears, cheers and champagne toasts with family and dear friends. Honeymoon plans would have been shared, along with my excitement and nervousness. I would have imagined gazing at my forever partner, smiling and feeling exhilarated about our moment.

Today, however, I lie here as one more day closes in this life we live, alone. I am not smiling. And while I may be hearing bells of the cathedral, I know they are the deep tones sounding from the wind chime nearby.

Life is funny, because as I lie here, comforted within the cradling arms of Mother Earth, it is with the knowledge that the life I once lived will never be as it was. My last glimpse of the Colorado sky I grew up admiring was beautiful, even still and soothing. Peace fills my soul allowing me to truly release, to let go, of all that makes up this life. My life.

After spending the day in my private refuge, contemplating how I got "here," I think back to my roots, to my parents, as they lovingly repeat their theory of love, even if just in my memory, with eyes wide open, and a broken heart, knowing this wretched sickness has taken my life.

No, I am not sick.

Let me tell you how it happened.

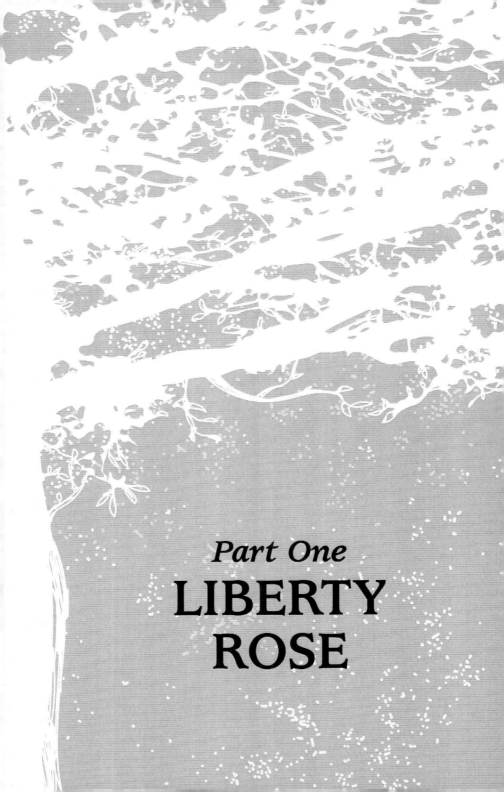

Part One
LIBERTY ROSE

IT WAS DURING A DASH OF TIME, the swell of a new season, a new promise; or so I thought. A paradigm shift, signifying my life was about to change. Adam and I, well, we were engaged to be married. To celebrate this new milestone of our life together, we went on a nine-day tour of Italy. It was such a great time, I thought, walking around the cobbled streets of Rome, driving through Tuscan villages toward Siena, the beauty of Siena itself, riding bicycles in and around Florence—*ah, Firenze*—taking the train to Venice and the ferry to the island of Murano, where the most stunning glass art is made. It was beautiful. The many slices of life we got to see, and even be a part of via conversations in broken Italian, or even with simple smiles, were something I believed would become a part of our life, together. When we made the decision to travel to Italy, I was excited about the trip, and mostly about the rest of our lives together as husband and wife.

Husband.

Wife.

Husband and wife.

The words now sound almost Daliesque; surreal.

Adam is my best friend, the man I have been with my entire adult life. As best friends, we have seen and done so much together. Our life has been a fantastic adventure. It was appropriate that even this moment would be marked as an adventure. The anticipation I felt, for the ringing in of a new day, was the eco-friendly energy

I have been relying on for every happy feeling since the day he asked me to marry him. This trip would signify the beginning of many milestones, and many adventures to add to the ones we had been blessed to have as a "soon-to-be" married couple. Italy was a beautiful and perfect location at which to mark this beautiful occasion. Looking back, I wish I could say our relationship was just as beautiful, amazing and perfect as Italy was.

Our relationship has always been a strange question mark. That is not to say it was not amazing, or beautiful, because, as in the old roads taking one into and out of sleepy Italian villages, or the antiquity of San Marco Square, or the artifacts found in hidden pockets of Rome, it is easy to see there was something substantial in our relationship that made our life together significant. When I look at who we are, together, it is beautiful and amazing, as well as fucking complicated.

A few months ago, I finally completed my master in Pacific international affairs and was promoted to director. Adam was given a cool new project with the company he worked for, and all was right in our slice of life. This was our new season, with the new promise of moving forward with our lives, as real adults. We had been talking about a plan to get pregnant within the next few years.

I really want a baby, to be a mom.

I really want to be a wife.

Being the planner I am, I thought it would make sense if we spent the next few years "living" as husband and wife before focusing on a new adorable baby.

Wait! I know what you must be thinking. Two people, engaged, one promoted to director; what about growing her career before becoming what is the label—?—ah, yes, before becoming "institutionalized." Is director as far as I, a free-thinking, feminist-minded woman, want to advance?

Is that my limit?

What about Adam?

You might be thinking, why is this chick forcing this dude into marriage, family and all that jazz? What about him? Is this what he wants?

I would be thinking the same thing, except for one key point: Adam and I have been together for thirteen years and engaged for a little over one of those years. After all the many ticks of the clock that had tocked, it was time. My career was on track and solid; so was Adam's.

Some would say, it was past time.

WE MET WHEN I WAS TWENTY-ONE. Adam was twenty-two. We were attending Colorado State University, in a town we both loved, Fort Collins. We loved the proximity to things we enjoyed doing, like backcountry hiking, quick day hikes and camping. It was also near enough to one of my other favorite mountain towns, Jackson Hole, Wyoming.

At the time we met, Adam was studying biology and I international relations. We were both considering a transfer to a different university, before we met. When we were sharing our stories of why, our reasons for transferring had nothing to do with not liking Fort Collins; rather, we wanted to see what life would be like outside of Colorado, where we had both grown up. Adam said he wanted to go to a school in Southern California, and I was undecided.

My hesitation was simply, I hold firm to my belief that Colorado is pretty fucking rad. I love the many opportunities to enjoy nature that are abundant here, the intense winding trails leading a person into moments of self-realization and purpose; the stillness of life when the snow falls, or when you are deep in the heart of the backcountry. It doesn't hurt that my parents are nearby. They are my other best friends. My other thought was Hawaii—hiking *and* ocean, that's pretty cool too.

Quality of life has always been important to me, and where I choose to live is a huge part of that. A humble yet vibrant life is what my parents provided for me, and what I want to provide for myself and for children of my own. Of course, relocating to a different school was about more than mere location. I wanted to find something that would give me a competitive edge when it came to looking for a job, which meant I had been looking for a school with the best reputation in international relations, with a caveat, the school also had to be located in a place where I would be willing to live, within a community I would want to be an active part of. After all, isn't that what makes life worth living? Being part of a community you love and want to make better? Yeah, I get it; sometimes the place you choose to hang your hat is just about the sacrifice, "the thing" which makes people stay in a place that isn't quite their own. All of that is fine, *but* there has to be a plan to get out and attain the quality of life that makes a person prosperous. The thought of becoming "stuck" was what made my decision tough.

It was a frigid Friday night in February 1993 when Adam and I met, when he sat at my table. Technically, it wasn't *my* table, and nothing about this evening was sultry or romantic, but I was sitting there, and then, so was he. Okay, an admission: my friend Kingsley and I had been sitting at this table for at least an hour. We left it for a few minutes when we stepped outside to enjoy a 420 moment, a moment of internal bliss. When she and I returned, he and his friend were sitting at our table. Trying to make small talk, mostly staking a claim to the two seats on the opposite side, I smiled and said, "Hey, you're sitting at our table."

He looked at me and, without even a smile, stoically replied, "Yeah? Well, it's our table now."

When I say stoically, I mean, no smile in his eyes, his mouth, no glint of joking around. I looked at his friend, who I knew from around the dorms and other parties, and smiled. He gave me that look, you know, with one eyebrow cocked upward, as if waiting to hear my witty comeback, but I was silent. Actually, thinking back, I found the moment unworthy of a comeback. I remember, Kingsley and I looked at each other and giggled before sitting at the opposite side of the table, facing the direction of the crowd to see what else was going on in this little dive. I thought he was a bit of an asshole, and we didn't talk at all for the rest of the evening.

That next week, between classes, I was walking into the school library while reading a review my instructor had given my paper, which was called "Globalization and the Potential Impact of Human Interaction in a Local Setting." I wasn't paying attention, and we almost bumped into each other.

"Whoa! Watch where you're going."

Startled, I looked up, then smiled at him. "Hey, it's you! Sorry about that." I raised my paper as if to redeem myself from my clumsiness. "Instructor criticism," I said. "Are you between classes, too?"

Again with the stoic face, he slowly rolled his eyes, glancing toward the library entrance.

"Uh, yeah," he replied.

He made me feel like an idiot for asking the obvious, because why else would one go into the library during the middle of the day, if not between classes?

"Yeah, of course, all right, see ya."

That was all I could say. I briskly continued on before noticing we were both walking across the foyer and toward the same elevator. When the elevator door opened, we both stepped in, and as my luck would have it, we were the only two who did so. It was awkward. I tried to avoid looking at him and smiled most peculiarly, which made me feel even more uncomfortable.

For the remainder of that semester, a similar thing happened, where we would walk into the library at the same time. There were a few occasions when I would actually show up at the library later than normal in an attempt to avoid seeing him, but it didn't matter, because he would seem to have been doing the same, and we would walk up at the same time. Eventually, it became less unpleasant. In late April, early May, we actually skipped going into the library and sat in the courtyard, talking. We talked about everything. Finally we introduced ourselves to each other.

"So, we haven't exchanged names. I'm Adam; you are?"

"Liberty. Liberty Rose Anderson. My friends call me Libby."

"Liberty Rose. How did your parents come up with that name?"

"Mmm, my parents named me after a principle and a right they firmly believe in. Liberty is 'the state of being free within society from oppressive restrictions imposed by authority on a person's way of life, behavior, or political views.' I'm not sure I live up to the honor of my name, but I do try. Rose is my grandmother's name. My dad's mother."

"It's beautiful, Libby."

Adam went on to tell me that, right after high school, he had made the decision to join the navy. He was based in Southern California; Tustin, actually. He found it sentimental to return to his birthplace, as he had been born near Tustin, but raised in northern Colorado. For Adam, it was like going full circle from birth as a child to a rebirth as he stepped into adulthood. He had just returned home in time for Christmas, using the time before the semester began to find a cool place to live. He had not been here long before the night we met in the bar, after being away for four years. He had earned a full ride to college. While in the navy, it appears, he met a girl he was serious about, who was going to school in Louisiana. He was really into her. After graduating from college, he had planned to meet her in California. They had broken up over spring break.

In my mind, this explained why he had acted so uninterested in me earlier and why he was so nice now. In my heart, it made me trust him, thinking he was not the kind of guy to cheat on someone he was dating. I quickly got over his rudeness.

I told him about my parents and how they had chosen to raise me outside of Telluride, on a beautiful southwestern Colorado haven. I had been homeschooled, and I described the societal outings my parents, and some parents of the other kids', would schedule as part of our community-building lessons. Most of which included hiking, camping and caring about the paths we take to reach our summit, or even our resting place. Our parents used these experiences as metaphors for succeeding in life. Truly, I like how my parents raised me.

We talked daily, though we never went out on a date until after the semester ended. There were no shared moments over coffee or beer or anything other than our courtyard chats or talks as we walked into the library. Adam simply didn't ask; nor did I—ask Adam. Looking back, our date would not have happened if my friends, Kingsley and India, hadn't invited me to go out with them. It was the last day of the spring semester and an end-of-semester bash was in the mix, complete with music, drink specials and free entrance for the female kind.

Funk-a-dunk was the band of choice and they were playing at a hot spot called "The Trail Stops Here." "The Trail," as we called it, was our local dive, and while nothing elaborate, it was a great place for of-age students to buy cheap beer and play pool, foosball or darts. While it was not fancy, it can be said it was all of the great people who shared moments at "The Trail" that made this dive special. It was a great place to listen to live music. Funk-a-dunk were from the northeastern USA, the homeland of this great country of ours—or so one story begins.

When the girls stopped by to pick me up, I was wearing a soft white long-sleeved cashmere sweater, cut-off jean shorts, tights and Birkenstocks. Although I thought I looked cute and was ready to go, Kingsley and India thought differently. They forced me to change my clothes into something they called hot and I called desperate. I hated it.

"Libby, you're a beautiful girl. Men are blind; you have to find a way to stand out so you'll be noticed."

"That's right, Libbs. It isn't healthy to maintain relationships with books only. We come to college to flirt and have fun. Let's find you someone fun to hang out with this summer."

India pulled from her bag a long-sleeved cornflower blue and white polka-dotted silk shirt and a dark cocoa-brown corduroy mini-skirt that zipped closed on the side. The polka-dotted shirt had ruffles and was cut low, "to show off the goods," she said. She was prepared to dress me it appeared.

Kingsley attempted to curl my hair, but I stopped her before the curls became too much. Instead, I tousled my long hair lightly and braided a small section in front, pinning it to the side hoping it would draw a person's eyes away from my "goods" and up to my eyes.

With hesitation, I relented and allowed myself to be clothed as a desperate girl looking for a desperate guy, and exchanged my Birks for heeled brown boots. The reason was selfish really; I simply did not want to miss the band, and fighting with Kings and Indie over what to wear would take me away from the start of the show.

When we entered The Trail, music was blaring from the jukebox speakers. The Funk had not yet started playing, which made me happy. Kings and Indie straight-lined it toward the foosball table to chill with guys I classified as "not my type." After a few minutes of checking out the scene and not finding what I was looking for, I went to the bar hoping to grab a seat so I could watch the band play. As if just in time, the band members walked onto the stage and started to play. They were awesome!

A few moments after I had sat down on the barstool, I heard someone with a thick Texas twang say, "Hey girl, can I buy you a drink?"

It was startling to hear that twang, and I slowly turned toward the voice. I saw beside me a tall, lanky man, leaning on the bar, smiling a Cheshire cat kind of smile, just standing there, attempting to look sexy. He was talking to me.

Unfortunately, I cannot say what he looked like, because he was wearing a huge Stetson cowboy hat that took up all of his personal space, which felt like an intrusion into mine. The big smile, the Stetson and the twang were all I witnessed. His teeth were sparkling white, and his voice was quite melodic. He was cute, just not what I was looking for. He would never have understood my family, much less me. Hating how I was dressed, and seeing the type of person hitting on me, I decided, indeed, I needed a drink, a stiff one.

"Um, yes, please. Thanks. Hmm, how about a double shot of bourbon and cola, with a lime on the side?"

The man with the twang looked at the bartender and tipped his hat. The drink arrived within seconds. Then the smiling man spat out more words that ruined the sound of the band.

"This band sucks," he said. "Whaddya say we leave this joint and go on down the street and do some two-steppin'."

Turning to him, I said, "Two-steppin'? I don't even know what that is."

We both laughed, and as he started to explain it, I cut him off.

"This band is pretty awesome, you know? I don't want to leave. Besides, I'm with my girlfriends."

Pointing to Kingsley and India, I noticed the loudness and excitement as they were disappointing many would-be suitors with their winning foosball pocket slams. The two of them, together, were unrelenting when it came to foosball. They never lost, and their wins were always rewarded with the drink of their choice, not to mention the guy of their choice. Returning my gaze to the twang man, I simply pointed out a fact.

"They would kill me if I left without them."

I smiled and thanked him, then pulled the glass closer to me and squeezed the lime into the drink. I turned to watch the band play. I vowed to leave the drink alone until this guy left, which was not happening as quickly as I had hoped.

A minute or so later, I heard another voice. "Hey, is this your drink?"

I turned and saw the stoic face of Adam as he pointed to my glass. Internally, I was joyously celebrating this intervention to rescue me from the twangy man in the hat. As I turned, I noticed Adam was looking at the low-cut drape of my outfit while smiling. Yes, I felt like a polka-dotted clown solely available for entertainment purposes. He was wearing a blue T-shirt over a white long-sleeved shirt, tan shorts and Birkenstocks. He looked cozy. I looked at the drink, then at Adam and, as stoically as I could, said, "Yeah, it's my drink. Why do you want to know?"

"You know, alcohol is the worst drug out there."

Adam sat down on the barstool next to me and leaned on the bar, relaxed, smiling. He stretched out his long legs toward my stool, like a cat marking its territory.

"Oh yeah? Why do you say that?" I asked.

"Well, I can give you three reasons. One, it's legal. Two, it's socially acceptable, unlike pot. Three, it's readily available; all a person needs is an ID with a legal age stamped on it. Kids can even get a hold of alcohol by getting a fake ID, sneaking into their parents' stash or into the stash of someone else's parents or family members. If desperate, they can always find someone to buy it for them. A person can easily become addicted, and because everyone else is drinking, it's hard to recognize when one has become an alcoholic, especially when you have become one yourself."

I looked at my drink, then at him, and chuckled. Before I could counter with anything in reply, he asked, "So, are you going to drink that drink?"

"Um, no?"

"Do you mind if I do?"

We both laughed and I said no, pushing it toward him. In turn, he bought the next few rounds. He sat at the bar with me, and we eventually turned toward one another. We talked, laughed and listened to the band for the rest of the night. I have no idea what happened to the man in the hat, but I suspect he chose to prey on some other sweet *somethin'*. When the band finished playing and it was time to leave, we walked outside and waited for our friends while the bar cleared out.

It was a beautiful spring night. There was a light breeze, which made it feel a little nippy; typical Rocky Mountain spring air, something I was completely acclimated to. Even so, I started to shiver. Longing for the warmth of cozy cashmere, I wished for my long-sleeved white sweater. Slowly, I wrapped my arms around myself.

"Are you cold, Libby?"

"Yes, starting to get there."

Adam took a step closer to me, as if to create body warmth. He didn't put his arm around me, nor did I put mine around him, but we were comfortably close. My heartbeat quickened, and suddenly, I felt so much warmer. His body was so close, I could smell him. He was wearing patchouli oil. The energy between us was so intense I could feel him, as if we were two magnets pulling each other closer. The buzz from our conversation in the bar, and all I was thinking and feeling, drowned out everything else. For a few moments, we were the only two people outside. Eventually, people started to exit and get into their cars. Headlights were turned on and shone right on us, like spotlights. As we moved away from the light, Adam asked me out, on a date.

"Hey, Libbs, do you like science?"

"Yes. A lot. Why do you ask?"

"There's a science fair at the Science Center in Greeley tomorrow. They will be opening a time capsule from fifty years ago. Would you be interested in going with me?"

At the time we met, Adam had long, beautiful blond hair that gently grazed his shoulders. His eyes are stark blue, like the deep ocean waters I surf and swim in. It was easy to get lost in them. He looked into mine and smiled. I smiled back.

"Sure. That sounds like fun. What time?"

I was excited about the possibility of hanging out with Adam, because over the course of the semester, I had grown to like him. If I am honest with myself, I am kind of a nerd, and people like me don't really get dates easily, not with people like Adam. Adam is hot. Tall, athletically fit, with a chiseled jaw and soft lips. Really, he should be with a cheerleader type of girl whose first name ends with an *i*, like Kandi, not with one whose nose is usually in line with the spine of a good book. Even though I was excited about the date, I maintained my composure while we finalized arrangements.

Our friends showed up, and as we each started to walk away, we turned to look back at each other. We smiled, and paused, as if we wanted to say, "Wait, what are you going to do? Right now?" But we didn't say that. Instead, we smiled and I said, "See you tomorrow." I flicked up my hand with a five-finger wave, and he hoisted a peace sign. Perhaps it was the phase of the moon, or simply the direction of the wind; whatever it was, as we moved away from each other that night, I knew I was in love with Adam.

The next day, I drove myself to Adam's place and parked. The hood to his car was up, and he was bent over, fidgeting with something. As I walked toward him, what I noticed first was he was not wearing a shirt. It gave me a chance to really look at his body, which I believe was his intention. His long, lean, muscular back was exposed. He was 6'1" and every limb was toned with muscular curvature. He was beautiful, incredibly so.

The temperature was going to be in the midseventies that day, and I was wearing shorts, a sleeveless shirt with a sheer loose pullover sweater to protect my arms from the harshness of the sun and, of course, my favorite Birks. The sweater slid gracefully to leave one shoulder exposed. As I drew closer, I called out to him and smiled.

"Hey, Adam."

"Hey, you found the place!"

He beamed a smile at me, walked over and gracefully, albeit deliberately, placed his wet sweaty armpit on my clean exposed shoulder to hug me. I returned the hug.

"Yeah, it wasn't difficult. Hey, is my car okay parked where it is?"

As he looked back at my car, I glanced at my shoulder and rolled my eyes at his sweat on my clean skin; yet, I didn't want to touch it by wiping it off. I surrendered to the moment and let it air-dry.

"Yeah, it's fine where it is. Uh, let me wash up and we can leave. Would you like to come in?"

"Yeah, sure. Is your car okay?"

"Uh, yeah, I was just checking some stuff."

"Ah—"

He gently closed the hood, and we walked toward his front door.

Adam, from the time I met him, was a frugal person. He lived in an apartment complex, in a seemingly shady side of town, away from the university. There were only thirteen single-story apartments in the complex, and Adam lived in the last one, apartment number 13. It was pretty cool, actually. The shape of the apartment was quadrilateral where the diagonals of the walls made a square, but two walls were longer, like a trapezium, which made the square look funky and the apartment larger. It was also the best apartment of the complex as it was on the corner, quiet, and had a lot of open window space for nifty peeks at the Rocky Mountains. If I believed in superstition, I would have thought the apartment number, 13, was creepy, but I wasn't, I am not, superstitious.

I rubbed my finger on the apartment number. Who knew the number, 13, would mark the number of years we would spend together? Should I have been more superstitious? Should I have walked away? Probably not; fate has its own way of presenting itself, so they say.

Adam went into the bathroom to wash his hands, and I started to look around. For $250 a month in the 1990's a frugal college student was living pretty easy in this nine-hundred-square-foot apartment. It had one bedroom and one bathroom and even had a living room, kitchen and small dining room. It was definitely larger, and cheaper, than my shared dorm room.

On one wall was a collage of photos of fun days gone by and people I assumed he had loved once, maybe still. There were photos of Adam rock climbing at Joshua Tree, California, again shirtless, exposing his strong back, and a photo with a friend giving a thumbs-up at South Padre Island, Texas, over spring break.

There was a photo of a girl posing, tauntingly, wearing nothing but a fatigues shirt, his fatigues, with his last name sewn on the shirt from his time in the navy. I assumed she was the Louisiana girl he had met in Cali. She was very pretty.

He walked out of the bathroom, dressed and ready to go.

3

THE SCIENCE FAIR TOOK PLACE in Greeley's City Center. The whole town seemed to have turned out to witness this once-in-a-lifetime event. Many booths were set up, where locals gathered to sell their handmade crafts, organic butters and preserves, as well as organic goods from their personal gardens. Local artists brought their wares, paintings, clothing, jewelry. Musicians from the region took turns performing, entertaining folks with cover songs, awesome guitar solos, and some of the best jams you'd find in northern Colorado. Everything seemed timeless and happy, which was the objective, I am sure.

The time capsule festivities began with greetings and accolades from the mayor, the director of the Science Center and the chair of the local women's club. After the last speaker, there was a stir of excitement as it was finally time to open the time capsule and expose the contents. At the risk of sounding like a cynic, I have to say the items in the time capsule were things one would expect to find: a black comb, a note from some young elementary-age student about how happy he was in his lifetime, a newspaper clipping with the date on it, and so on. It was somewhat anticlimactic.

Seriously, I don't know what I was expecting. It would have been 1943 when they put items into the time capsule and closed it. Maybe something iconic from surviving the Dust Bowl or the Great Depression; I don't know, maybe even a relic from the old

Colorado mines, a wagon wheel or a newspaper clipping with a photo discussing why a woman was seen doing a man's job while the men were away fighting in World War II, yet was unable to buy a fucking house on her own without a man's permission. Perhaps, even, a law from the law books firmly expressing that a woman was the possession of a man, but a donkey had the right to choose what would be placed on its back for towing. Histrionics, I know. I guess I just wanted to see how fortunate I was, as a young woman, fifty years later; but, whatever, a comb would do. It was, after all, a fifty-year-old comb. It was also black, just the way I like my coffee.

Afterward, we drove back to Fort Collins, and enjoyed dinner at the Mexican restaurant called Chicas, where so much tasty grog was consumed, I simply couldn't drive home. The safest, most responsible thing to do was to spend the night at his place; at least, that was my logic at the time. So, I did. It was fun. I mean, I had fun. The next morning, as we lay there in his bed, we looked at each other and smiled for a moment before wrapping ourselves around each other, practicing our own version of the Milton Bradley game, Twister. Of course, there wasn't anyone spinning the arrow on the board, or calling out which appendage should land on which colored circle; rather, we were merely making our own twisted moves, which would allow us to fit within one another perfectly. After *it all*, he turned to his side, facing me, and with that damn stoic facial expression, he asked, "Do you regret last night or this morning?"

I abruptly looked at him with a certain curiosity, a level of shock, as if the neural relay in my brain was bouncing between synapse and dendrite, as if the dendrite was blocked from the synapse, thereby creating a level of confusion. While I was surprised by the question, I pondered it for a moment and then said, "No."

"No? Why not?"

"Because, Adam, I am not the kind of person who has sex with *just anyone*. I am cautious about whom I choose to share myself with. In fact, you are my second. Besides, it's not like I just met you last night and then we had sex; we've been getting to know each other throughout the semester."

"Yeah, but it was a first date."

"Yeah, and now I'm starting to regret it."

I began to get up, but Adam pulled me back to him as if someone had called out "right foot, red circle," and the heated Twister game commenced as our lips locked in a kiss.

A couple of days later Adam called, we went out again, and before I knew it, we spent the entire summer together. We went to a music festival, Lollapalooza, in Texas. We camped and hiked through New Mexico, Wyoming and, of course, Colorado. We spent every night together in his trapezium-shaped apartment. Three months after our first date, I moved into the funky shaped apartment, number 13, with him. Five months later, I moved out.

Living with Adam was easy, and a lot of fun, so he wasn't the reason I moved out. It was the way my father reacted that was tough. It came to light, while my father was pretty easygoing with true hippie values, he still held fast to the old tradition of courting, engagement, wedding and *then* moving in together. Traditions taught to him by his father. He was "highly disappointed" in me. To absolve myself, I used all kinds of logic, like, "It will save you some funds by not having to pay for my dorm room" only to have him retort, "What gives you the right to decide how I spend my money?"

"Libby," he said, "if you are moving in with Adam, please be honest with me, and most importantly be honest with yourself about the reason you are doing it. It's not about the money. The decision to move in with someone, or to be with someone for that matter, should never be about the money. Money may get you things, but it should never be the basis for the person you decide to become. Did Adam present this cost savings as the basis for you two to move in together?"

Both my father and my mother were big on the theory that people shape their lives based on the type of person they choose to be, which is reflected in the choices they make, the path they take. In this moment, I chose to break away from the mold to see if this was the kind of person I wanted to be.

"No, Dad. I understand you are pretty peeved, but look, I love this guy. I'd like to ride this out."

To show his adamant disapproval, my father stopped talking to me. When I went by to visit, he would say hello, give me a hug and then walk out of the room to "do something." If I called, he would hand the phone to my mother, after basic greetings and salutations. It was hard having the most important male figure in my life avoid me. It was unsettling. When it came right down to it, my relationship with my father was more important to me than determining if I wanted to be someone different. After carefully considering the implications of my moving out, including the possibility Adam might bail on the relationship, the decision was made that I would move out at the end of the semester. And after I moved out of Adam's place, my relationship with my father improved. All was perfect within my tribe, my home community, once again. Adam and I continued dating, and the decision turned out to be the right one.

Somewhere during that time, however, we found out I was pregnant.

4

IT TURNED OUT, WHILE ADAM and I were dating post-my-moving-out, he started dating another girl. He had taken her to meet his grandmother, whom I loved greatly. She was exactly five feet tall, had the most radiant smile and the most contagious laugh. She told amazing stories about her time as a child surviving the Dust Bowl, as well as the Great Depression, while living in a small Texas farming town; stories from the type of time I hope never to experience.

For fun, she read tarot cards and had taught me to read them on my own. I actually became quite good at it, though I do not have a deck of my own. Because of her tarot reading skills, Adam and the new girl went to her house, to learn their future together so they could validate every reason to move forward with living in bliss. It was during this reading that Adam found out I was pregnant and, with a phone call, how I discovered the pregnancy myself.

"Libby, it's me. Have you started your period?"

"What? Um, hello? What in the hell kind of question is that? You do realize you are calling me at work, right?"

My part-time job was working in a local dermatology office as an insurance file clerk. To avoid having others hear my angst, I put my hand over my mouth, covering it to prevent anyone else from hearing my very personal conversation. Why he couldn't have waited until I was home was unfathomable. Waiting, *that* would have been the mature thing to do.

"Libbs, I'm serious. Are you pregnant? Gran . . .uh, I need you to take a pregnancy test and let me know what it reads. Please."

His voice was soft, pleading, somewhat desperate sounding. It scared me a little.

"Fine, Adam, but I think this is weird. I'll take the test and will talk with you later tonight."

I gently placed the receiver back onto the phone set and looked around to see if anyone had heard my very personal conversation. Fortunately, no one was around. I then went back to work as if nothing had happened. Later, I took the test . . .six different times! Each little test stick gave the same result, "Positive." After reading each result, I checked the box for an expiration date. Each box was current. After calming down from my own personal panic attack, I called Adam and told him I was on my way over. He was waiting for me when I arrived. Without my having to knock on the door, he opened it and I walked in. I looked at his face, and without his saying anything I knew what he was thinking, which was, "Well, are you?"

"What the fuck, Adam? How did you know I was pregnant? This doesn't make any sense!"

He sat down on the sofa, closed his eyes, and covered his face with both hands, slowly letting out a deep groan. I proceeded to pace the living room. We were quiet for a few more moments before he gently said, "Are you sure, Liberty? Sometimes these things have a false positive. Maybe you should take another one. I bought a package."

"Adam, I took the test six fucking times. They can't all be false positives."

"Please, Libby, will you please take the test? One more time?"

Looking at him as if he must be mad and although I was deeply offended, I agreed to the "one more time," because, what if?

Together, we went into the bathroom, and he watched as I performed the deed. It was as if his standing there would change the result, similar to how when you have a technical issue, you call tech support and the issue seems to disappear. If only it were that easy. Ha! As we waited for the result, I washed my hands and asked him again how he knew I was pregnant. He proceeded to tell me about the other girl he was dating, how they met and, worse, how he thought she was "the one."

"Her name is Mandi. We met in a photography class. She's funny, as tall as me, and not at all like you. She's beautiful, elegant. We have a lot in common. She didn't sleep with me on the first date. We've been on several dates before having sex. She's awesome. I don't want to lose her."

That is not exactly all Adam said, but those clipped sentences about Mandi are all I remember. They cut deep into my breaking soul and they hurt, deeply. All I could do was sit there, motionless, listening as he went on to explain how he took her to his grandmother's house to introduce her.

"A few days ago I called Gran and explained how I thought I had found 'the one.' I asked her if I could bring Mandi by so she could read our cards. Mandi and I both wanted to see what the future held for us as a couple. Gran started to read the cards, looked at Mandi and apologized, saying she usually had a good read on me, but today all she could see was a family friend. Then she looked at me and said you were pregnant. After I took Mandi home, I called you."

At that moment, I felt a level of ridiculousness I had never felt before. I felt sick to my stomach, as if I could expel any food or liquid that filled my belly, or any baby seedling that was clinging to the inside of my warm womb. I felt weak. After baring all, Adam went into the bathroom to check the stick. I got up and started to pace again.

Trying to hold it together, I sat down on the arm of the chair clos-est to the door, closed my eyes as I got my bearings, only to open them and stand to gather my things. I walked toward the door.

As I was about to exit, I heard Adam call out my name.

"Libby."

I turned to him without saying a word; instead, I let my wide-open eyes ask the question, "What?"

"It's positive."

Closing my eyes, I turned toward the door, twisted the knob and walked out.

"Libby. Libby! Wait, we need to talk! Libby!!"

ALTHOUGH I COULD HEAR ADAM calling my name, I ignored him. At that moment, neither his voice, nor his sour logic, was what I wanted to hear. Instead, I drove around our little slice of northern Colorado for a long time before stopping at the lake overlook of Estes Park. I got out of my car and sat on the trunk, holding my knees to my chest while looking up at the brilliant stars of the night sky, and then down onto the lake, contemplating the rest of my life; contemplating the life of this child and what it would be like, as a single mother, to raise her. I sensed this child was a girl.

I cried.

Over the next week, I took the test four more times, on four different days, just to be sure timing didn't have something to do with getting a "negative" result. It was clear I was in a state of denial. The first test was taken as soon as I woke up and with the first pee; the second, right after lunch; the third, after work; and then finally, right before going to bed. Each time I was using different methods like pee a little first, then pee on the stick; then pee a lot, then pee on the stick; then pee on the stick for exactly fifteen seconds; and lastly hold the stick under the flow the entire time. The reading was never anything new, not even a false negative, and I was crushed.

Adam called me daily over the next week, but I ignored his calls. While there was a lot to talk about, I couldn't talk to him. Where would we begin? I was angry about the situation, but I did not want to talk, much less fight, about it. Then, one day after work, while walking to my car, I noticed Adam's truck was parked right next to mine. He drove an old Ford Bronco. It was gray, with a black pinstripe and tinted windows. He was leaning on the back of the truck, hands tucked in his two front pockets. Even with the bill of his baseball cap covering his eyes, he was looking miserable. I could not ignore him any longer.

For a moment, I paused and looked around to see if any of my coworkers were around, as I did not want anyone to see, much less hear, us argue about something so personal. These baby deets had not been shared with anyone, not my family, my friends, especially not my coworkers. I did not know what I was going to do: keep the baby or not. Slowly, I walked toward him, and before I could say anything he came up to me, put his arms around me and whispered, "Liberty, I am so sorry. Will you please forgive me? We can work this out, I promise. Let's just talk about it."

After a moment, I returned the hug, and we were back together.

About a week later, we drove down to my parents' place outside of Telluride to share the "news." It was the first time Adam would see where I had grown up, and the first time he and my parents would meet. The introductions went well, I thought, and I took the time to show Adam around. Over dinner was when we told my parents about the pregnancy, which did not go so well.

"So, Mom, Dad, Adam and I have something important to say."

"Oh, Karl, let's fill our glasses with wine. There may be a toast in order."

My father happily obliged, filling even my glass. I looked at Adam and we both smiled a supportive smile. I placed my fingers on the stem of the glass and gently swilled the wine and then, with both hands, cupped the glass. That wine glass instantly became my anchor.

"Well, as you know, Adam and I have been dating for a while now. Even after my moving out of his place, we have worked to continue our relationship. We really love each other."

"Yes, Mr. and Mrs. Anderson, I adore Libby."

My parents turned to each other and smiled. They were expecting an announcement about getting engaged. Knowing I was about to break their hearts, and as guilty as I felt about this disappointment to come, I remained strong. Clearing my throat, holding my wine glass more tightly, I smiled and spilled the news as delicately as possible.

"So, the important news is, somewhere in all of this time of getting to know each other, and falling in love, we have found ourselves pregnant. I'm pregnant. Adam and I are really excited about our baby and our future."

It was as if I had spilled the glass of red wine on my mother's antique table runner; the one given to her by her mother, which had been passed on to her by her own mother and her mother before her, which would ultimately pass on to me and to my child. As expected, my parents flipped, especially my father, essentially telling me I had failed.

"What? What are you saying, Liberty?"

He stood abruptly, pushed his chair back and began to pace. His hands seemed to go everywhere. First on his hips, then one hand reached up, cupping his mouth, eyes closed, eyes opening, and then his fingers ran through his long blond locks, rubbing his scalp as if to feel this moment as real. Time passed without anyone saying anything. I had never witnessed this type of anger coming from my father. It was startling. He turned to look at me, then at Adam, then back at me. His eyes shot through mine, like gun eyes, and I looked to Adam and then back to my parents. My father turned to my mother, who was looking at him. Their expressions were like a mirror image; both were truly disappointed in me.

"Hell, Libby, you haven't even finished your college education. You haven't allowed yourself to experience your potential as a young woman in your career or in this world. You haven't even discovered who you are as a person."

Then they both looked at me, and my father started to say something but covered his mouth before running both hands through his hair once more. There was silence for a few minutes before he belted out what he had been waiting to say.

"For crying out loud, Libby, you haven't even made your mark. How in the hell are you going to be able to teach your child based on what you have learned in your lifetime so far? You're still a kid yourself."

Standing, he leaned his weight forward on the back of his chair. To emphasize his point, he lifted the chair and abruptly set it down, creating a banging noise. The loudness startled me, and I jumped a little. A few drops of wine splashed on my hand, and I let go of my anchor. He then stared at Adam with a most hateful look.

"And you, who in the hell are you? Why are we just now meeting you? What kind of a man are you? You live with my daughter for a while, she moves out, and now she's pregnant? Are you planning to marry my daughter?"

My father's tone and words were harsh. Adam and I were speechless. My father stopped talking and turned away. He poured my mother and himself each another glass of wine. Adam took my glass and swallowed the contents in one swoop. We were all silent. The funny thing was, my father wasn't wrong. My mother supported my father's outburst, and I couldn't dispute any of his points. All I could offer was, "Well, Dad, what do you recommend I do?"

It was a childish response, I know, but the disappointment my parents were experiencing was so heavy, my childish logic was all I could lean on. My father looked at me with his brilliant blue eyes, and snorted. No one said anything more. After excusing myself, I got up from the table, leaving Adam sitting with them, only to leave the house and walk to the creek, alone. I needed a quiet moment with nothing but the trickling sounds of the creek. I hoped the soothing sounds of the flowing water, and the crisp mountain air, would mellow this moment.

Over the next several weeks, I began to relay the news to Kingsley and India and then to my boss at work. The more I started to let people know, the more tense things became between Adam and me. We started to argue, we stopped talking with each other and when we did talk our conversations began with Adam repeating, "Libby, I think we should get an abortion. It's the right thing to do."

"Oh, really? You do? And why is that, Adam?"

"Because, Libby, we don't have anything to offer the kid. We're college students for fuck's sake! I'll have to drop out of college to support you and the kid, and I'll resent you both as a result. I don't want to do that."

"Um, then don't! What happened to 'we can work it out,' Adam? Why are you bailing on me now, after I've told my parents, my friends and people I work with? I cannot have an abortion now, not after telling everyone I know!"

"Sure you can, Liberty! You can say you had a miscarriage. That happens, you know."

"Adam, you're missing the point. This is a personal matter, one I shouldn't have to explain to anyone."

"We can have another baby, Libby, later, when the timing is right, when we have something to offer, like a home and, I don't know, *things*."

"Oh my God, Adam! Really? Things? No! I cannot abort this baby! If we hadn't told anyone, I would consider it. But now? Now, everybody knows."

"My God, Libby, who cares what other people will think? Seriously, it's just you and me here, right? If any of this, whatever you and I are, is to work, it's gotta be just you and me. Please, tell me that's the case."

"Seriously, Adam, abortion is supposed to be a personal, private decision. If I have one now, it is no longer private! Why didn't you say something before?"

"Because, I thought we could handle it! Now, I'm not so sure I can."

"You don't have to stick around, you know. I am willing to sign a piece of paper to absolve you of any obligations."

This went on for weeks; yelling, arguments with Adam, arguments with my father, and then, I lost it. What I mean is I lost the little seedling clinging to my wet, warm womb; like, no more baby in my stomach. It was done—kaput, finito, and no more reason for anyone to argue about a baby that no longer was.

I cried every day for months, and fell into a depression. In my heart and mind, I hated Adam and wanted nothing to do with him. I was also angry with my father. I swore I wouldn't talk to him until I could accept what had just happened, and I secretly worried that time would never come.

I was twenty-two and all I wanted was to finish my degree so I could move on. The spirit of this baby filled my heart and mind with the deepest desire to live a life fulfilled, for the two of us. This milestone would be a key contributor in my becoming the woman I was supposed to be, for her. I swore I would not let the memory of her be insignificant.

Everyone, including Adam, wondered how I lost the baby, but I didn't talk about it with anyone else. Holding tight onto my memory of that moment, I will just say this: whether it was by choice or by nature, losing the baby was a heartbreak, a mindfuck and painful. It was also no one else's business.

Love.

Love is so fucking complicated, as is life, because there are so many different ways to love, and to live. You show your love by being kind, even if it is simply with a smile and a wave. You are courteous and respectful of others because of love. That is, simply, kindness. You love the earth because, like the tit for a baby, or umbilical cord to the fetus, it is what feeds and nourishes us; the foods we eat, the water we drink, the air we breathe. Mother Earth is our connection to all of that which we are: a soul free to wander in all that we see with our waking eyes. The earth is our foundation, our grounding.

Love is like the blood in our veins, and the air we breathe; it is sustenance.

There was something about Adam that made me fall in love with him, over and over again, and it was this. He had a vulnerable side he rarely let anyone see, a side that would just pull you into him. He could be caring, and kind. When I lost the baby, I attempted to isolate myself, to get away from Adam and my father. But Adam ended his relationship with Mandi, and he wouldn't let me out of his sight. Every day he would bring me lunch. Before leaving me, he would show a goofy smile, which would make me laugh a little. Sometimes he would bring me a plate of fresh-cut bananas and strawberries with a daily dose of a multivitamin tucked beneath the last piece of fruit. It was clear he was trying. He took care of me, made sure I was okay and encouraged me to get my head back on straight. And I let him. In a way, I felt I needed him to get through this sour time in my life. I told myself that only he understood what I was going through.

I realize now, we were the wrong shade for each other from the beginning. We should have walked away from each other at this marker in our lives. Before walking away, we could have looked back at each other, like before, smiled, paused, as if we wanted to say, "Wait! What are you going to do, right now?" Instead wave good-bye before turning to walk away knowing it was the right thing to do, for us both.

If we had ended the relationship, we both might have found Mr. and Mrs. Right.

If we had, I wouldn't be sitting here contemplating my life with the potential effects of this illness.

6

THE FALL SEMESTER FINALLY BEGAN and I was more eager than ever to get the semester completed as well as my degree. I made the decision to stay at CSU to avoid wasting time. That semester, and going forward, I decided I would not be living in the dorms. Too much had changed, and I simply desired peace. Really, I needed to be able to focus on my future, sans interruption from dorm-room antics. My parents didn't refute my decision, and together we looked for an apartment. My parents agreed to furnish it.

The apartment I admired most was in a fourplex built in the 1920s. The only apartment available was on the second floor, on the left side of the building, which faced south and was a mere five to seven minute drive, or bike ride, to the school. The building was in an eclectic bourgeois section of town, and apartment availability in this neighborhood was rare. The apartment number was a single digit, 4. We decided I should take it. The floor was covered with a nasty green carpet, which I asked to have removed and replaced. The owner, who also lived in the building, in apartment number 1, agreed to this, if I paid for it myself.

The apartment was beautiful, with floor-to-ceiling windows that let in the most amazing light. In the dining room was a full wall of built-in book shelves, and there were original black and white hexagon floor tiles in the bathroom. In the living room was a faux fireplace, complete with mantle. I loved the antique style of the apartment and agreed to pay for the replacement of the carpet. However, when we pulled it up, we found the most amazing wood flooring. Rather than cover it with carpet, Adam, who was still in my life, graciously volunteered to sand the floors and finish them with a gorgeous clear varnish. I was in love with my new home, which carried a righteous rent expense of $325 a month. For me, this fresh little apartment made the sordid loss of my baby a tad less unbearable.

Adam followed suit and moved in with me one month later. My parents didn't argue with me about this. I suppose it made them feel better knowing I was not left to myself to brood. Life with Adam wasn't perfect, admittedly. Neither of us was the same after our loss. We slowly started to grow distant from each other, becoming more like roommates. I focused on school, and Adam did the same. Our interpersonal interludes became less frequent, and he began staying out late. I didn't consider it an issue because I took on a new part-time job, working late evenings at a market research call center in Loveland. One night, late, Adam came home after drinking with one of our friends; I had already gone to bed. He was a bit toasty. He leaned over to kiss me on the cheek. I thought he was going to whisper sweet somethings in my ear and that we would commence our little game of Twister. He did whisper something, but sweet it was not. It hurt my feelings.

"You ruined everything, Liberty. I just want you to know that."

I had no idea what he meant. Was he blaming me for getting pregnant? Or for losing the baby? Was he blaming me for his losing the girl he thought was "the one"? I didn't know and I didn't care, even though the comment stabbed through my soul. He kissed my forehead, pulled away and began to leave the room. Rather than reacting, I simply said, "Thanks for letting me know, because

I have been staying awake wondering. It's been taxing my mind, you know? But, now, I can finally go to sleep. Good night, Adam."

A few weeks later, as I was washing dishes, Adam came up behind me and hugged me. Neither of us said anything; we both embraced the moment. Adam was the first to break the silence.

"Libbs, we should go out, on a date. We haven't done that in a while. Interested?"

"Could be fun. What do you have in mind?"

"Maybe ditch class, go on a hike, then happy hour at The Trail? We can play darts, hang out, then go catch a live band? What do you say?"

"Sounds like fun. It has been too long. Friday?"

"Friday's perfect."

Adam kissed my hair, hugged me again, and then left the kitchen.

The date started out with a big tasty breakfast: eggs, turkey bacon, steamed rice and white country gravy. It was a perfect day for a hike. Fall was definitely in the air, which was a bit crisp. As we walked along the trail, we told stories and laughed about stupid things we had experienced since the "situation."

That is what it had become, a situation. Neither of us could call it what it was. For me, it was like a tainted stain on the palm of my hand, like that of Lady Macbeth. The spirit of that soul I'd lost remained embedded within my own soul. A permanent indication of my new core self, with her spilled blood tattooed on my palm in invisible ink that only I could see, over a scabbed wound in my belly only I could feel. Adam never brought up the subject, and we have not really discussed it. Sometimes I wondered, did he know, much less care, what really happened?

At our summit, we sat to enjoy our cinnamon sprinkled peanut butter and banana sandwiches and water. The view was as it always was, beautiful, peaceful. A snapshot of all I love about Colorado. I'm not sure what I love most about reaching a summit after a climb, the magnificence of everything that can be seen, the valley below, the expansive lakes appearing as small as tubs of water, or the peace that comes from the humble gratitude of being a part of something so intricate. The Rocky Mountain breeze tousled my hair and kissed my skin, reminding me that I was loved and eventually I would be all right.

After the hike, we took a shower together, and after *it all*, we opted for a short nap before going out. It felt good being next to my best friend again, lying in bed, snuggled within each other, hands clasped; it had been a while. That was my first relaxed sleep since I'd lost the baby.

We left for The Trail. Adam invited a couple of people he knew to happy hour with us. They met us there. That was the first, and only, night I met them. I was having fun until Adam disappeared. It didn't really dawn on me he was missing because we knew a lot of people in this little place and I was chatting with all of those I knew. It had been some time, and it was great to see friends in this setting. Kingsley and India were still flirting with the boys, trying to win a chance to play foos and ultimately take control of the table. We hugged and chatted for a bit. As they focused on their game, I continued chatting with other people from the dorms and from classes that were shared.

Ultimately, I found myself back at our table with other people I knew. I looked for Adam, but didn't see him. Instead, there was a strange man sitting across from me at our table, and his blank stare started to make me feel uneasy. He kept looking around, completely unfocused on what we were talking about but focused, for sure, on his sister who had met us here. It was an uncomfortable feeling, being around this guy. Each time I tried to talk to him, he would look at me with a "you disgust me" sort of look, and then he would turn away without saying anything. I thought it was weird.

Looking around the table, I suddenly realized I did not know anyone else sitting there. It was as if my friends and I were playing musical chairs. I got up to get another beer and made the decision to locate Adam, but Adam was nowhere to be found, neither inside the bar nor on the outdoor patio. I figured he must be in the men's room, so I walked back in that direction, thinking I would just wait, and then deciding I was ready to leave. Leaning against the wall, I was thinking just how fun the day had been. Time with Adam had been conflicted with unresolved emotions. The day spent hiking and laughing together assured me that we might be able to continue our connection, until I saw something that made my heart sink into the pit of my stomach.

The bathroom doors at The Trail have privacy glass windows. Windows frosted white, which prevents one from seeing behind closed doors, yet allow one to see a silhouette. According to the owner of The Trail, it was the easiest way to know if someone was in the bathroom without having to knock obnoxiously and thereby disturb someone else's business. It was an interesting point of view, I'd thought, hesitantly, when she explained it. Standing on this side of the privacy glass, I was grateful for her logic now, because the silhouette I saw was of two people kissing and having what looked like raunchy bathroom sex.

I simply could not believe what I was seeing.

I gracefully knocked on the door.

"Busy!" Adam yelled out.

"It's me, Adam. It's Libby. I'm ready to go."

Hearing my voice, I surprised myself with how calm I sounded. I leaned back against the wall for support as I waited for Adam to come out. While I was waiting, there were muffled, frenetic words that sounded like:

"Oh shit, shit, shit. We've gotta go."

"Who's Libby?"

"Ahhh! Come on, hurry."

He walked out of the men's room smoothing his shirt and ensuring the zipper of his shorts was fastened. At the sight of this betrayal, I was left speechless, flabbergasted, disappointed. Actually, I was fucking angry. I looked at the girl; she was somewhat pretty. Worse, it was the girl who had met us there. She apparently had no idea Adam and I were living together, much less a couple, at least not based on what she said next.

"Heeeeyyyy, it's you! Libby, right? So, are you ready to go catch that band?"

Letting out a perturbed "right," I looked back at Adam with my meanest look, my attempt at making "gun eyes." I took a deep breath, hoping this moment would disappear, but it didn't. They were standing there looking at me, each with different expectations of how I would react. I started to walk "off the trail," so to speak. When I turned to leave, there was the creepy brother blocking my path. This time I had nothing to say to him, not even a pleasant smile to give. I looked away and walked out of the bar. My plan was to walk home before I realized how ludicrous that idea was; home was too far away.

Going back into the bar, I stood in front of Adam, slapped him hard across the face and said as calmly as I could, "This Jerry Springer bullshit does not happen to me. You will drive me home, pack your shit and move out."

I didn't yell. I think only Adam was able to hear what I said. He started to say something, and he might have slapped me back, but restrained himself when my friend Matt came over while maintaining eye contact with Adam. Matt simply asked, "Are you all right, Libby?"

Adam responded, "Who in the fuck is this guy?"

Matt was 6'4", bald by choice, Black Flag–listening, black-leather-wearing punk friend from my youth whom I highly valued. We had been homeschooled together, sort of. What I mean is that all of the homeschooled kids in my community had play day twice a week. This was when the parents would socialize with other homeschooling parents, and when the kids would have a chance to socialize with other kids their age. We would go on nature hikes along different trails, or someone would host a kid gathering. It was always fun. Matt was cool when we were kids. He introduced me to punk music, which was different from the folk and trippy hippie music my parents listened to. Matt was still cool and also going to UNC.

Matt inched closer to Adam, holding his pool stick in hand. I noticed out of the corner of my eye that all of the guys Matt was playing pool with also had bald heads or Mohawks. They placed their drinks down and, while strategically holding their pool sticks, slowly inched toward us. Because of my friendship with Matt, I knew every one of them, and I was grateful knowing I had friends who would protect me, if it ever came to that. This was not that time. Matt and his friends would have hurt Adam, badly. To prevent further Jerry Springer camera-worthy action, I assured Matt I was okay.

"It's all right, Matt. Adam isn't a violent guy and doesn't believe in hitting women. He's going to drive me home, right, Adam?"

"Right."

Matt backed off, looked me squarely in the eye as if trying to gauge what I wasn't saying. I smiled at him, trying to assure him

I was fine. We turned away and Adam drove me home. Truth is, Adam wasn't violent, so I wasn't lying to Matt. What I wasn't saying, however, was I was wholly embarrassed by Adam's disgusting bathroom activity I had just been made privy to. It suddenly made me wonder just how much of a habit this dirty bathroom antic was when he went out without me. It seemed so natural for Adam, considering I was right there, in the same place. On the way home, the conversation was the most ridiculous I have ever had.

"You do realize, Libby, I was going to get a tattoo tonight?"

"Um, really, Adam? You do realize I was excited about our first date since . . .I don't know, uh, since our convoluted dash of fucked up time."

I was horrified he was more upset about not getting a tattoo than about this betrayal. Not even an apology for embarrassing me in front of people, especially people I knew. Nevertheless, I was curious.

"As if it matters, what were you planning to get?"

"It matters, Libby! I was going to get a turtle."

"Aaaah, a turtle? Right."

"Yeah, it symbolizes Mother Earth."

"Well, it's not too late. Once you drop me off, you can do whatever you want. And whomever."

"Well, I can't get a tattoo anymore. You ruined it."

I looked at him, suddenly realizing I didn't know Adam at all. I then looked away from him. It was dark out. The light that illuminated each passing stripe from the headlights of Adam's car, and the sound of the rotating tires on the pavement, helped create a mellow cadence that was a nice pause in this warped moment. That is when I laughed.

"What's funny?"

"Me."

"Yeah, how so?"

Rather than reply, I simply shook my head as if to say, "It doesn't matter." I turned to look out of my window, into the darkness, while Adam drove me home, the whole time thinking how stupid I was for believing we could ever work things out.

When we arrived home, he walked me up the stairs. We entered the living room, and he looked around at the space for a long moment, before reaching out to grab the green vase on the mantle. He released it so it smashed into pieces on the floor. Then he looked at me, his eyes hollow. I jumped. For the first time, I was actually afraid he was going to hit me. Quickly, I braced myself and prepared for a hit. Actually, I don't know if I would have even known what to expect. I have never been hit by another human being.

"If you don't mind, Liberty, I'll come by in the morning to get my things."

"Whatever, Adam; tonight or tomorrow, really, I don't care, as long as you're out."

He left. The only violence was Adam's childish act of dropping my vase on the floor. With tears streaming down my cheeks, I swept up the remnants of the vase, a small symbol of our broken dreams, our shattered relationship. I took a shower and went to bed. As hurt as I was, I was more livid at my stupidity, and I couldn't wait for Adam to be out of my life.

7

THE NEXT MORNING, the doorbell rang. When I answered, I saw
that two of Adam's friends were standing there.

"Hey, Libbs."

"Heeeyy, what's up? Adam isn't here right now. Shall I ask him
to call you, or go by?"

"Yeah, no, we're here to see you. Matt told us about last night.
We wanted to make sure you were okay. Are you all right?"

Matt lived in the dorm room immediately across from theirs.
He knew these guys were friends of Adam's, and I am sure Matt's
concern was the basis for this visit.

"Ahh, sure, come on in. Yeah, I'm all right. I am just so humiliated."

"Have you eaten anything today?"

"No, I don't have an appetite."

"You should eat something. You're going to need your strength."

At that point, Adam's friends took me for breakfast at my favorite eatery, Daffodils. What made Daffodils so fantastic was their
outdoor patio. Pots of colorful geraniums, lavender, and begonias were
arranged perfectly around the tables. Each table had its own bright
yellow umbrella, which could be opened or closed as one desired. The
place was clean, colorful and beautiful. In a word, the atmosphere at
Daffodils could be described as "happy." The food was pretty tasty, too.

As we were eating, I shared the gritty details of the night before.

"So, do either of you know this girl?"

They looked at each other.

"Tell her, Al."

"Yeah, she is my ex-girlfriend. We broke up several months ago. She lives half a mile away from Adam's mother's place."

Again, I felt ridiculous. Over the past month, Adam and I had been going to his mother's house to visit on weekends. She and I would mess with her garden; Adam would go on a bike ride. At times, he would leave me alone with his mother for hours. During this confessional, I realized Adam would have been riding his bike to this girl's house. My mind reeling with the image of their silhouette from the night before, I could only imagine they were doing more than just talking.

"Thanks, guys. I appreciate you telling me the truth. So, Al, are you all right? Did you dig this chick or something?"

"Yeah, completely, until now."

They took me back to my place, and I thanked them for breakfast. There were no signs of Adam being in the apartment, so I started to pack his things for him. About an hour later, I received a phone call. It was Adam's mother.

"Libbbbeeee, baby! I heard about what happened. Are you okay?"

Adam's mother said my name long and drawn out, slowly, as if she were saying it while exhaling a breath.

"Yeah, I'm all right, just humiliated, disappointed and very angry. I'm sure Adam has told you I've asked him to move out?"

"Yeah, honey, that's why I am calling."

"You know I love you," I said, "but this relationship is not going to work out. Adam and I are really over this time."

There was a brief pause before she continued speaking.

"Can't you just stick it out a little while longer, at least until the semester is over?"

Was I really hearing this? Had Adam asked his mom to call me?

"Adam has nowhere to go, Libby. He gave up his apartment when he moved in with you, and he can't stay here. It's too far away. You two live so close to the university. Adam loves you. We love you."

There was a long pause before I replied. I was beside myself with weird amusement and exasperation. I felt like I was participating in a warped Claymation version of my life.

"Fine, but he has to sleep on the living room floor. Not the sofa, not my bed, but the living room floor." Like a dog, was what I wanted to add, but I couldn't, not to her. She had always been sweet to me.

"Ok, Libby, thank you. I will let him know."

About an hour later, Adam came back to the apartment. We didn't talk for a few days, and against my better judgement, we were still living together.

8

FOR THE REST OF THE FALL and spring semester, Adam and I stayed out of each other's way. He did exactly as I asked and slept on the floor. The floor was hardwood, sans rugs or carpeting. It had to be a miserable sleeping experience. I remember on the first night, I quietly tiptoed into the living room to check on him. It appeared Adam had created a bed of sorts using his camping mat and many layers of blankets and sleeping bags. Really, my only concern was I wanted to see whether he had snuck up onto the sofa, like an unwatched dog. I was pretty pissed and was determined to make sure he suffered. When I saw him sleeping on his makeshift bed, my heart melted, but I didn't relent. I wanted him to suffer for being such an incredible, indelible asshole.

Fortunately, our class schedules were different. My classes started as early as 8:00 a.m. most mornings, and Adam's began closer to 10:00, which made living with him all right. After several weeks, I started to wake him up on my way out the door as I left for class, only to tell him he could sleep in the bed. A month after that, I told him he could sleep in the bed with me, as long as he didn't touch me. He still continued to spend late nights out with who knew who, or what, and each night I worried he would end up in some drunken accident. When I would hear his car drive up, I would allow myself to go to sleep.

One night, I heard an engine roar, tires screech across the road and finally metal crunching hard. It was around the time that Adam would normally come home, so in my heart and mind, I knew the car was Adam's. In haste, I threw a sweater over my pj's, slipped into my Birks and ran toward the sound, all the while praying every prayer for Adam's safety. Though I was angry, I still loved him greatly.

As I got closer to the car, I noticed it wasn't Adam's, and I immediately began thanking God. What I also noticed was the car was on a slight upslope of the hill and had tried to go through the solid pine tree, which had stopped the car by almost splitting it in half. The driver's door was open, and a man was hanging out, one arm almost touching the ground and his head resting on his shoulder. It looked as if he had tried to make a mad escape but was being held captive by his seat belt. Praying a new set of prayers, I checked for oncoming traffic. When I saw there were no other people or cars coming toward us, I quickly ran across the street to see what was up.

"Hi. I'm Libby. Are you all right?"

"Yeah, I bumped into a small tree."

Smiling, I moved the man's hair out of his eyes.

"Yeah, I noticed that. Do you feel any pain?"

"Nope. You're beautiful. Are you an angel?"

"Um, have you been drinking?"

"Yeah, a little bit."

Don't judge me, but I looked around him and noticed there were three empty beer bottles on the floorboard. In that flash of time, I made the decision to throw them away. This guy was hurt, and what I thought was most important was he receive the medical care he needed, and maybe a traffic ticket, but not be held in a jail cell until he was sober and then taken to a hospital, or vice versa. My rationale was he would be suffering the next day and for many months after, possibly years, and that was enough.

"You have open containers in your car!"

"Wha?"

Not wanting to hear him make excuses or deny the obvious, I interrupted.

"Yeah, look, I am going to call an ambulance because you need help. Before I do, I am going to take your open, empty containers and dump them in the recycle bin over there."

Pointing to the blue bin by the fence, I asked if he had any other open containers. He said no. I also asked if he wanted me to call any family. Again, he said no. I stood up to leave.

"Thank you, Angel."

I blew a kiss, then ran to the bin, dropped the bottles into it, and then ran back to my place. I started to hear sirens, and I knew someone had called the police. I also dialed 9-1-1, just in case the sirens were for something else. An hour later, Adam came home. Because of the night's activity, I was still up and somewhat frazzled. I was sitting on a chair in his "bedroom," my living room, reading. When Adam saw me, his face lit up. He smiled and, while putting his keys on the table, tried to start a conversation with me.

"Hey."

He said it with such vibrancy. I smiled in return, and without saying anything, other than a return "hey" in a flat voice, I got up, headed for my bedroom and went to bed. We had essentially become estranged roommates who shared a bed during the remainder of the fall and spring semesters.

Finally, classes ended and the anticipation for summer was starting to build. I was looking forward to a break. Adam had packed his bags and waited for me to return from work at the call center to tell me he was moving to Las Vegas, Nevada, where his grandmother now lived. She had moved to Nevada for the sun and the benefits that she, a widowed, AARP-card-holding senior citizen, could reap. Adam had cleaned the apartment and made it appear as if he had never been there. He made dinner that night, and we toasted the end of the semester, the end of us, with a bottle of cheap drugstore Cabernet.

"Hey, Libby, thanks for being so cool and letting me stay here these last two semesters."

"Yeah, it's been a long road. So, you'll be going to Nevada!"

"Yes. I've been talking to Gran; she has agreed to let me live with her for the summer. I am going to try to get some work in one of the casinos and save some money for next semester."

"That's a great idea. So, when do you leave?"

After I said that, I realized it sounded callous, rude and definitely cold, but that was what we had become to each other. I smiled, somewhat embarrassed by my response. Adam chuckled.

"I deserve that. Leaving tomorrow, first thing in the morning, or, if you'd like to drive with me? I can wait until you get some time off. My treat. What do you say? It could be fun."

"Maybe. Let me think about it."

The next day, I agreed to drive with Adam to Vegas. I took time off, and we drove away in his fully packed car.

The emotional distance and hurt between us had dissipated; we were friends again.

9

THE ROAD TRIP TO LAS VEGAS took ten days. We allowed detours as if we would never be in these places again, at least not together. We explored the Painted Desert and the Meteor Crater site of Winslow, Arizona. The Meteor Crater itself was cool. It's about one mile wide, 560 feet deep, and the impact was made about fifty thousand years ago, according to our tour guide. It was the first time I had seen anything like it. If you are ever near Winslow, Arizona, take a moment to go see such an awesome phenomenon. We also went out of the way to stay at our favorite camping and hiking grounds in Colorado and New Mexico while we discovered new ones near Flagstaff, Arizona.

Eventually, we arrived in Vegas. The feel of the desert air on my skin was different from anything I had ever felt before. It was cleansing. Seeing Adam's grandmother again was great. She looked refreshed. We spent every night in different casinos playing craps or blackjack until we were silly drunk from the free cocktails provided to us by the skinny, barely clothed girls, who would happily serve us. Three days after arriving, Adam and I drove to San Diego, California, then trespassed into Baja California, Mexico. We drove until we decided to stop, which was how we ended up in Ensenada.

The stoplights at the intersection were a mind boggle in that, from our vantage point, we could see both a green light and a red light. It was hard to decipher which one was ours, the light closest to us or the light on the other side but still facing us. We both started to laugh.

"Um, which light do we pay attention to?"

"I'm not sure. Logic would say the one closest to us because it's closest to our lane."

"Yeah, but Libby, they are both facing us. The road is in the shape of an X, not a plus sign."

The lights switched colors. We looked at each other and laughed some more. We then looked in all directions; there were no other cars coming. Nothing in sight, no activity whatsoever.

"Just drive, Adam. Let's get to a hotel. It's dark and getting late."

Adam drove forward and immediately some red and blue lights started to circulate. We were being pulled over by the Mexican Policia. We laughed again and said, "Shit! Where did he come from? Do you have any cash?" The officer walked up to us with his flashlight shining toward our faces.

He started to speak in Spanish, which neither of us could understand well. In my broken Spanglish, I attempted to tell him we were looking for a hotel. He asked for our driver's licenses. We provided them and he returned to his car. Adam watched him through his side mirror and noticed the officer was laughing hysterically. Once the officer had composed himself, he walked back toward us and, in perfect English, said, "Excuse me, did you notice you passed through a red light?"

"Really?" Adam looked at the officer innocently and replied, "It was difficult to tell which light was ours."

"Look, there is a Days Inn close by. If you go straight to that hotel, I will not give you a ticket."

He pointed toward the hotel and gave us detailed instructions on how to get there. The officer was friendly, very nice. The streets were dark, and it was a puzzle to know if we were heading in the right direction, but lo and behold, there was the hotel, bright and inviting after the last turn. We checked in, tuned in to Mexican television to see what the locals occupied their nighttime with, took turns showering and then slept. The next few days were spent exploring the city of Ensenada and the people. It was a great time. Baja California in the nineties, so fun, so safe. Sometimes I wish we could go back to the simplicity of that time. We considered driving deeper into Baja, but instead we turned back toward the States and to Vegas, where I spent the rest of my vacation lying by the pool and absorbing the rays of the sun for the most amazing suntan.

Somewhere in this time slice, Adam found a way to kiss me, and we became a couple again, at least during the time I was with him. Truthfully, we never said we were a couple, yet we never said we weren't. The matter was left unspoken, just like everything else we had been through during the last couple of years. At the end of my little vacation, I bought a ticket to fly home. Before I went into the terminal, Adam and I paused to look at each other, face-to-face, for what felt like a brief escape into our own private bubble. We embraced, foreheads touching, fingers woven together, lips close enough to brush against the other's. We didn't let go until there was nothing more to say.

"Libby."

"Adam."

"Thank you for coming out."

"It was fun."

"You should know that I love you. You do, don't you?"

"Maybe. I'm still trying to figure that out."

"Well, you shouldn't have to figure it out. I love you. I always have. That's what makes it so hard to leave you. Unfortunately, I keep hurting you, and I don't know why, because you are the last person I want to hurt."

"Yeah, well, I wish you would stop, because you're killing me, Adam. Seriously . . .killing me."

We stood there for a few more moments in silence.

"Look, I'd better go."

He hugged me tightly, kissed my forehead and my lips. I returned the kiss, and afterward, I looked at him, smiled, and slowly our fingers unlaced.

I walked away.

10

A COUPLE OF WEEKS AFTER I returned home from Las Vegas, Adam called me and we started to talk every day. He apologized for his deplorable bathroom engagement, for Mandi and the way he handled the whole pregnancy, especially after telling my parents. The only thing we did not talk about, was the loss itself. But, we took the time we needed to get to know each other again, albeit over a telephone wire. There were calls when I did all of the talking and Adam listened, and vice versa. There were emotional moments, and eventually we forgave each other.

We were each other's best friends, and we realized during that summer we might be able to make a future together. When we were able to talk without being emotional, he invited me to come to Las Vegas again, and I drove out to visit him once or twice a month, spending at least one week before driving back home. Thank God for summer jobs as a student and the free time that could be negotiated.

During one of my drives back home, outside of Gallup, New Mexico, along the 40, I noticed a girl standing on the side of the road with her thumb sticking out. She had shoulder-length blond hair, wore sunglasses and what looked like a long-sleeved button-up shirt and an ankle-length skirt. I remember thinking, either I, a fellow sister, could pick her up, or some weird truck driver rapist/ killer would. So I pulled over. She ran up to my car as I cleared the passenger seat for her.

"Hey! Thanks, are you going toward Taos?"

The chick, it turned out, was a dude.

"Um, I thought you were a girl. I don't have anything to steal."

He smiled and said, "I don't want to steal anything, except for a ride. I'm on my way to the Rainbow Festival in Taos."

If you don't know, the Rainbow Festival is a hippie thing where like-minded individuals gather together to live in an all-natural kind of commune in the mountains. This is where different groups do what they are good at, like making an oven out of mud and eating foods captured via fishing, hunting or other foraging techniques. If there is one thing I do trust, it's a peace-loving hippie, and I trusted this man instantly. Turned out, the skirt was actually a pair of some serious bell-bottom jeans. They had to be a thrift store find. I smiled.

"Sure, hop in. Where are you coming from?"

"California."

"Yeah? I love California. Are you from there?" I asked.

"No, from Georgia, actually, Atlanta," he said.

"Hotlanta! That's cool. Were you in California for fun?"

"Yeah, Hotlanta." He laughed and then continued, "Some friends and I drove out to follow the Grateful Dead. It was a great time until my car died."

"That's a bummer. Where are your friends?"

"They stayed behind. I am hitching my way back toward Georgia. That's where I am going to school. Thought I'd camp out at the Rainbow Festival for a while before the semester begins. Have you ever been?"

"No, but I've heard about it."

"You should come to this one with me. They are a lot of fun, definitely a great experience."

"I totally would, but I have folks expecting me."

In truth, there was no one expecting me except for Adam who was waiting for me to call him saying I had made it home safely. Taos was a couple of hours out of my way, but I drove the Dead-head hippie hitcher all the way there, and we chatted about school (he was an engineering student), life (it was made for living) and music, not just the Grateful Dead. He was pretty cool, and we had a lot in common. Once we made it to Taos, I stopped to get some gas and snacks. Taking in the splendor of this mystical place made me think of my parents' magical homestead, and I decided to drive to their place to stay the night.

When I was growing up, my parents and I lived on several acres of land in southern Colorado with our nearest neighbor at least two miles away. This was the land I would be driving to from Taos, where I always drove when I needed to think, and it is where I am today, recounting my life with Adam, from the day we met to now, trying to figure out where in our relationship timeline we could have caught this virus.

11

SITTING HERE, IN THIS TREE on my parents' refuge, overlooking the beauty of the San Juan Mountains, I can remember the first day I heard about AIDS. It was a Saturday in the late 1980s. I remember, because I was waiting to watch, *Style with Elsa Klensch* on CNN. It was a Saturday morning favorite, as I love fashion, even though I am not fashionable. That show is no longer on the air, and I do miss it. The newscaster was recapping the headlines when he made a simple comment, "There is a new epidemic that has scientists, and the CDC, baffled. The disease is called AIDS. Anyone can get it. There is no cure. In other news — "

I remember wanting to know more about what this meant. When the story actually hit home was in the 1990s. That is when a community AIDS testing facility opened in Durango, Colorado, for all area residents. The test was free and anonymous. Not knowing anything about AIDS except for what the newscaster had explained, I walked into the facility and asked to take the test and learn more about it. I remember a roomful of people as young, and not as young, as I, waiting to do the same thing. Hanging from a wall was a quilt. Each square represented people from our area who had died from AIDS. There were so many squares. The quilt covered the wall like a multicolored mural. It was almost unbelievable, considering I hadn't heard about anyone dying of such an incurable sickness in the papers, or on the local news.

George Bush, the original, was our president and the first person I had the opportunity to vote for in my young adult life. If you ask me today why I voted for this man, I will return a blank stare in answer to your question. I think our voting preference is supposed to be private and not worn as a label. Nor should we pin onto our lapel, like a badge of honor, the words "I VOTED!" because that just makes one look like a pretentious fuck who is clueless about what they actually voted for. The "I voted" sticker tells the world you are like a sheep used as bait to tempt the wolf that is coming in for the kill, the wolf being the financial backers and/or the party we actually voted in. The "I Voted" sticker is a brand saying you "belong" to something. Belonging is good, if you know to what it is that you belong, and why.

Don't get me wrong. I am thankful for the right to vote, especially as a young liberated woman knowing how many women before me fought so hard, not only to vote, but later to be able to purchase a home without the permission of a man. These are things I refuse to take for granted, things I will fight for in the spirit of the daughter I lost, and for other young women who will come after me. I believe everyone, of and over the proper age, should take time out of their day to do the needful.

In truth, at this moment, I've forgotten why I voted for the original President George B. It doesn't really matter, not anymore, because as I sit here, in my favorite tree, my personal thinking log, what matters is the test result, then, was negative.

As this cool mountain breeze brushes back my hair, kissing the skin of my face, making me feel loved, I admit I am afraid to learn what this new test result will be and what the rest of my life will mean. As I inhale deeply, I attempt to gather the building anxiety if only to exhale it all out so it will dissipate into the air, and into nothingness.

12

THE TREES IN THE GROVE can block any view of the mountains, but most of the time, the majesty of the Rockies will present itself and humble me. My dad built a beautiful home for us, including a typical red barn, which he filled with horses, chickens, pigs, a cow and a goat. We also had two sweet English springer spaniels who followed us everywhere. They were spoiled, and unlike the rest of the pets, they slept in the house, on their own cozy beds situated right next to my bed. They passed away several years ago and are buried in the family plot.

Our house is less than one hundred feet from a little creek that gracefully skirted the land. My mother and I created stepping-stones out of colored pebbles and cement to make a path from the house to the creek as part of an arts and crafts project during homeschooling. Three of the stepping-stones have our handprints cast and dried into the cement, complete with our names, as well as the dates on which we were born. All of the stones have shaved mica rock scattered at the top and dried in. This was to give us light at night as the moon, or our flashlights, reflected off the mica rock shavings. Of course, the light wasn't bright by any means, but there was a sparkle, which made our trail easy to see when light shone upon it.

The water in the creek is numbingly cold, but the trickling sound is peaceful. There were nights when my mom would take a blanket, call on us to follow her and lay it down close to the creek bank. We would lie there in silence. The sound of the creek was mesmerizing and the stars above us beyond words. If you have not taken a moment to stargaze, you should, especially when there is a meteor shower; these are absolutely breathtaking, albeit humbling.

At this moment, I can hear the creek trickling, performing its duty as called by nature, and I can't help thinking about my life on this refuge, starting with my mother. She has always been a spectacular force in my life. My time with my mom is one of my favorite things. The sound of her sweet voice always seems to calm me, the gentle touch of her hand grounds me.

Among all of our pets, aside from our dogs, my favorite was my collection of rabbits. I loved to pet them. They were soft, like velvety silk. There were five. My dad helped me build an amazing chicken-wire-walled home for them. The home stood three feet off the ground, which protected them from any type of predator who might break in solely to enjoy them as lunch or a midnight snack. Their stilted platform condo also prevented the rabbits from burrowing underground into a path that would lead to my mom's organic garden in an attempt to plunder and pillage the innocence of her prized garden. That happened once. My mom was wholly distraught.

"*Liberty Rose Anderson!* Look! Just look at my carrots! My kale! Ooohhh! How are we going to eat?"

When I ran to see what her frenetic cries were about, I stopped and hid behind my father, who had also run to see what caused her outburst. We stared at her, at her garden, wide eyed and speechless. The rabbits had destroyed her would-be harvest and I felt horrible. She complained every year after when it came time to prepare for the next planting. Each new planting was sentimental, with a tear and a prayer in memoriam for the patch prematurely destroyed by those blasted rabbits. My daily chore, from that point forward, was to keep the rabbit condo clean. They could go anywhere with me, into the house and around, just as long as I ensured the rabbits were secure, *away* from my mother's garden.

My father's name is Karl; my mother's name is Sarah. They do not work typical office jobs. At least they don't anymore. Before I was born, my parents had careers. They traveled around the world and invested wisely. Together, they earned and saved enough money to sustain their lifestyle for the rest of their lives. They had a life plan, and when it was time to have a baby, I was conceived. They moved from San Francisco to southern Colorado before I was born in an effort to ensure the innocence and simple pleasures of life would be instilled in me. That was when they bought this land and started to build on it. That was thirty-four years ago. The house is beautiful with amazing custom features my father crafted on his own.

My parents are not simpletons, although they lead a simple kind of life. They are simple in that they do not act like the kind of people who have money. As a matter of fact, I didn't know my parents had money until I was older. My dad's hair has always been long, shoulder length, thick, shiny and blond. His blond hair, always parted close to the middle on its own, is touched with brilliantly natural sunflower and honey highlights that glisten regardless of which way he turns. Like me, he has the bluest eyes. What I love most is he has the happiest smile and the best laugh. His warm, gentle, patient personality is the hallmark of our family. In the summer, he can be found sporting a simple pair of shorts, short- or long-sleeved T-shirt and Birkenstocks. In the winter, it's jeans, a sweater and closed-toe Birks.

My mom has the same peaceful demeanor and beautiful, happy smile. Her hair is a lustrous milk-chocolate brown that stops above her waist, like mine. She always wears a dress or skirt with a shirt or sweater, even when she is out gardening, even in the winter.

She once explained soft dresses or skirts make her feel feminine, and she loves that feeling. Her garden is beautiful, organic and well maintained. It has always rewarded the family with a plentiful bounty during the summer and in the fall. Anything in excess is canned and stored for winter, shared with neighbors, or sold at the local farmer's market. My parents have found a way to live off the land and from the animals in their barn: eggs from the hens, milk, yogurt and cheese from the dairy cow and goat, meat from all, except the dairy cow, if so desired. Sometimes, they trade chicken for beef. In the winter, my dad hunts for elk or deer to enhance our protein selection. For grog, my dad brews his own beer. The first toast of a newly brewed batch is always the same.

"This is for you, President Carter. Thank you!"

This toast, my father will attest, is because President Jimmy Carter signed a law permitting a person to brew beer at home, which is so rad. Jimmy C., the prez, was a great president, most definitely my favorite. My father and mother built a water collection system to collect rainwater, or snow in the winter, to water the grass instead of using water from their well. They created and maintain an awesome compost collector. We live a self-sustaining life. Maintaining this lifestyle is a chore, definitely a job in and of itself, but we always have had enough and wanted for nothing.

Many years ago, when I was around nine, a young couple stopped by and the young man knocked on our front door. My father answered and went out to talk to him. My mom and I wondered aloud to each other, finally admitting we did not know the family. It turned out, the young man was passing by with his wife and they needed a place to live and work. He saw our gate was open and took a chance we would be able to help. He asked my dad if he could help maintain the land, the animals and whatever needed maintenance in return for a place to live and food for his family. Seizing the opportunity, my dad obliged. That night, they set up camp down the path, next to the creek. The next day, my father and the young man began building a cottage on the other side of the barn, out of our line of sight, so each family could have a sense of privacy when the sun started to set and the day came to a close. The family, the Upchurchs, became a part of our family, and soon, they began to emit the radiance of my parents: happy, peaceful. They live here to this day.

Every morning, my mom would lead us all on a short hike to her favorite part of the creek and would direct us into perfect yoga poses and meditation before homeschooling would begin. If it was during the winter, she would direct everyone to practice our poses by the big sunny picture window looking out onto the beautiful San Juan Mountains. Once yoga was over, she would send me to dress for the day, and when I returned, there would be melt-in-your-mouth delicious smashed banana, blueberry and walnut pancakes for breakfast. To this day, I continue to practice my mom's yoga poses each morning, but I have never had pancakes like hers, anywhere.

My parents are amazing. They really love each other. At times, I will catch a glimpse of them as they talk. They look each other in the eye and flirt as if they are still in the early stages of dating. My father will gently place his hand against the small of my mother's back and kiss her on the cheek, and she'll blush and smile or giggle. She always gives him "that" look, which simply states he is the only man she will ever love. It is beautiful.

My mom is like that with me, too, always gentle and kind. When I was younger, she would kiss me on the cheek, leaving behind a wet, temporary tattoo of rose-colored lip balm. Other times, she would stop to hug and tell me just how beautiful, smart and wonderful I was, always letting me know we were all so lucky to have one another, and this quality of life. Then she would send me along to do some sort of fun chore, like hike to the tree grove and come back with a story to share at suppertime. Because of this experience, I thought my life would be like that of my parents, and I would be married to a man who absolutely adored me, one I absolutely adored in return.

13

WHEN THE SUMMER ENDED, Adam returned from Nevada to CSU. He moved back in with me, and we both completed our degrees. On graduation day, my parents came up to Fort Collins to celebrate this momentous milestone with us. We all knew it had been rough. Looking back, I am so thankful I survived it and was able to maintain a pocketful of sanity. After the graduation ceremony, we all went to eat dinner in Greeley, where my father indulged us with pricey bottles of wine, delectable food and a champagne toast. Adam and his family were also included.

"Liberty Rose, our only daughter and child. You have been the sun, the moon and the stars to light up our sky. When we look at you, we know life without you would make our world an empty place. Today, you have reached one of many milestones in your young and beautiful life. Your mother and I are incredibly proud of you. Congratulations, darlin'."

With that we all raised our flutes to touch one another's and said, "Cheers!" I felt my eyes water and a tear stream down my cheek. I wiped it away and chuckled out of embarrassment from being such a sentimental sap.

"Thank you, Daddy. I love you!"

I stood up to hug him and kiss him on the cheek. I had forgiven my father a long while back and embraced just how much I loved my parents. At that point, I felt my mother take my tear-stained hand and squeeze it. We looked at each other, smiled and, at the same time, said, "I love you!" We gave each other a hug, and then my father began speaking, this time to Adam.

"Adam, I admit I was not keen on you the first time we met, considering the first time you and I met was when I learned about the pregnancy. That was not the way I imagined I would meet my daughter's future partner in life. As a matter of fact, I imagined I would not be meeting that person until Libby had a chance to explore the beauty, opportunities and successes that would pave her way to a fulfilled life. If I may, I wasn't sure you would still be here with Libby, after the loss; but, here you are, a college graduate, a man who appears to love my daughter and a man I look forward to learning more about. Congratulations, Adam! I am proud of you for reaching this important milestone. May this be one of many, and may your life be as accomplished and fulfilled as you deserve. Cheers!"

Again, we all raised our flutes, touching them with a clinking sound, repeating the word, "Cheers!"

I remember looking at Adam during that toast, smiling and knowing I truly loved him for everything we had been through and survived together. He had changed. I was proud of the man he was becoming and was excited about next steps. He had a look of hope and accomplishment. He smiled back at me and winked. That same weekend, our parents helped us pack our belongings from the apartment into a moving van, at least the things we wanted to keep. That which was no longer needed, or wanted, we gave to remaining students or donated to the local women's shelter. The rest of it would be taken in the moving van back to my parents' home and stored in my room. Adam placed his things in a storage unit and paid in advance for the full summer.

Once everything was packed, we drove our cars to southern Colorado where we spent a few weeks with my parents and the Upchurchs. Adam and I took some time to explore my favorite hide-aways, and my family had some time to get to know Adam. As planned, we loaded up Adam's car with our backpacks and bikes so we could travel throughout the western United States. The plan was to camp and hike in places we had never been before. We bought a large Rand McNally road atlas which showed many back roads to cool locations. The goal was to decide where to live next. During that summer, we drove through Texas from Amarillo to the German Hill Country and down to South Padre Island. We stopped at the famous Cadillac Ranch and camped in Palo Duro Canyon, took the back way down Highway 70 to Fredericksburg, where we camped at Enchanted Rock State Park. We went on to Port Aransas, where we camped right on the beach. Our first hotel stay, and indoor shower, was at South Padre Island. Texas is a beautiful state. We also summited Wheeler Peak of New Mexico, Mount Elbert of Colorado, Mount Whitney of California, Kings Peak of Utah, Humphreys Peak of Arizona, and we hiked to the bottom of the Grand Canyon. The canyon was hotter than I expected it to be, as well as more beautiful than I had imagined.

We also camped at Phelps Lake in the Tetons outside of Jackson Hole, Wyoming, where we encountered moose. The first encounter was with a female protecting her herd from a male moose. We hid behind trees and bushes, along with other hikers. It was beautiful. Our second encounter was at night, which frightened me a bit. Adam and I were eating dinner when we saw what appeared to be small lights walking toward us. We could hear the rustling of leaves and footsteps on the trail. As the lights grew closer, we realized they were glowing eyes. Of course, people say not to panic and to stay still, but the mind can trigger some real emotions, like panic! Which is what I did; I panicked and ran into the tent. Adam, of course, maintained his composure and followed the textbook advice to stand still. Within minutes, we saw a team of momma and baby moose walk onto the trail in front of our campsite and then divert up and away from us. They went by so slowly, peacefully. It was the most beautiful experience I have had. Once they passed, Adam and I laughed at my reaction, then cleaned up our food to avoid attracting bears, and then we crashed out.

In California, we drove north on the Pacific Coast Highway from Malibu. We stopped and toured the Hearst Castle and went through Big Sur, Monterey and San Francisco, finally making our way into Berkeley, which we both loved, before driving up into Oregon and then Washington. I believe I can say I have seen all of the western part of the United States, from Texas, New Mexico, Colorado and Wyoming to California, Oregon and Washington, and everything in between. It was the best time of my life right after college, and for me, it was another indicator we would have a life filled with adventure.

I was happy.

14

AS THE SUMMER DREW TO AN END, we started to drive back toward my parents' place where I would stay for a while, sending in résumés in search of a job. On our last night before going home, Adam and I decided to stay in Flagstaff. We checked into a hotel room, showered and went to a local bar to drink a few beers, listen to a band and play darts. Afterward, we walked to a restaurant to enjoy a nice dinner to close out our adventure.

"So, Libby, this is our last real night together. What do you think?"

"This trip has been so much fun, Adam. I am excited about our next adventures."

"Yeah, so where are you going to look for a job?"

"Hmm, after this trip, I have to say, Southern California. I fell in love with the coastal communities of San Diego. That place is beautiful. What do you think? Could you live there?"

"I'm not sure," he said. "I can't make up my mind. There is still so much I want to explore, on my own."

"Oh, well, I am a little confused. I thought we would be starting a life together. Isn't that what this trip was about?"

"Libby, I'm sorry. I didn't mean to lead you on. This trip wasn't about starting a life together. I wanted you to see there is more to life than the paradise where your parents had you holed up all of your life. I wanted you to see how other people live outside of Colorado."

"Wait, what? Are you trying to tell me this trip was about two people hooking up and exploring the western US and not a couple building a relationship?"

"My God, Libby, you have always been the person to read into things that aren't really there."

"Wait! What?"

"Libby, you and I both knew this relationship wasn't going to work after college. There is too much sordid history between us. We can't even talk about how you lost the baby."

"Why do you say that? You haven't even asked me about it."

"Ugh, I don't want to argue, Libbs. This trip was to see new things, experience new places and find a peaceful, mature way to end what we have."

"We can talk about the baby, Adam. I have nothing to hide from you. Just ask me about it."

"What difference does it make, Libby? It's not like it will change anything. Let's just call it what it is."

"Which is what, Adam?"

Adam opened his menu and ignored my question. I opened my menu and looked down, not reading at all, not knowing what to say, think or feel, other than, I'm an idiot.

"Libby, I love you. You are my best friend. We just can't work as a couple."

"You're right, Adam. Seriously, I don't know what I was thinking. I have my whole life ahead of me, and I am excited about how great it is going to be. This being our last night, let's enjoy it and tomorrow we will head home."

After saying that, I looked at Adam, and all I could do was smile, a guarded kind of smile to mask how I was really feeling. Then I looked back at the menu, this time considering my options for a meal.

We ordered hamburgers with steak cut fries and several pints of local ale and enjoyed dinner before returning to our hotel room to bid farewell to one another. (Left leg, green circle.)

The next day, we drove back to my parents' place. It was a long, quiet drive, with no more words said, the only words coming from lyrics of Fleetwood Mac tunes blaring from the stereo speakers. When we drove up to my parents' home, I saw they were cuddling and swinging cozily in the hammock. I could imagine they were whispering sweet somethings into each other's ears. Looking at Adam, I realized he would not be the man who would love me like that. How was it I had fallen in love with him? This man was nothing like what I had imagined I would have in a relationship. I chuckled lightly out loud.

"What's funny?"

"My parents."

We stopped the car, and as we were unpacking my things, my parents came to meet us. We all hugged one another. My father grabbed my backpack, and my mom grabbed Adam's hand and mine and pulled us into the house.

"I am so happy to see you both and cannot wait to hear about your trip. We're making dinner. You two go take a shower, freshen up and meet us on the patio. The Upchurchs will be joining us."

Obediently, we did as she asked and for the rest of the night, we talked about all of the amazing feats of our trip, or I should say, I talked and on occasion, Adam would chime in. We all sat around the table, drinking tasty wine, telling tales and laughing. Not at any time was it mentioned, when Adam left the next day, it would be the end of our relationship.

15

AFTER ADAM LEFT, I cleaned out my backpack, hung up my sleeping bag, and did laundry before unpacking boxes to get my room organized. Not knowing how long I would be staying with my parents or how long it would take to find a job, I wanted to make my room cozy. Besides all of that, it was the right thing to do considering this was my parents' house and not a storage unit.

My mornings continued with ingrained habits, walks to the creek for yoga, followed by amazing smashed banana, blueberry and walnut pancakes, or whatever breakfast concoction my mom placed before us. I picked up my chores and enjoyed being back on the Anderson family reservation. When I wasn't following embedded family rituals, I worked on my hunt for a job. As I had told Adam I would, I started my search in Southern California, and to my surprise, I quickly found a position working as an analyst in the International Relations Office of the World Trade Center in San Diego. It was another milestone, which made my father happy. To celebrate, my parents and I decided to fly to San Diego for a few weeks.

"Libby, darlin', do you want to invite Adam? We haven't seen him in a while."

"Ah, yeah, Dad, he won't be joining us in San Diego. He is actually continuing his backpacking excursion throughout South America."

It wasn't a lie. Adam and I were still talking to each other from time to time, and this was the last thing he'd said he would be doing.

"South America, huh? Why didn't you go?"

He was fishing for details, but I wasn't ready to tell him we weren't dating any longer, so I simply made a plausible excuse.

"Well, you know, job competition. I didn't want to miss out on an amazing opportunity because I was backpacking in South America, you know?"

"Uh-huh. Okay, well then, it's just us!"

"I'm excited, Dad. It's going to be a lot of fun."

"Hey, what do you all think of this new dress? Is it too touristy?"

My mom had flown up to Denver for a girls' trip with Mazy Upchurch and had bought a few dresses that were unlike anything she had ever worn. While all of my mother's dresses were simple, this new selection had a bit more flair, and all of the dresses were bare shouldered.

My father and I looked at each other, then at my mom, and we said, "Pineapple. Needs pineapples embroidered on the dress."

We all laughed and there were no other questions about Adam. After our touristy sight-seeing excursions, we spent the rest of our time in San Diego searching for the perfect place for me to live and getting me set up. My parents surprised me by purchasing a small two-bedroom condo in Pacific Beach. Of course it was paid for in full, using Anderson Family Trust money, which meant it belonged to my parents, though I had the opportunity to live there rent-free. My father called it a wise investment, one that would pay for itself in the future. I called it fucking cool!

16

THE NEXT SUMMER, one year after graduating, I heard from Adam. Turned out, he had called my parents, and they had given him my new number and told him where I was living. After all, why wouldn't they? My parents believed Adam and I were still dating.

"Hey, Libbs, it's me! I'm in San Diego and thought we could meet up for drinks, dinner and catch up on what's new in our lives. Give me a call. Here are my digits—"

That was the voice-mail message he left. He didn't say his name, but I immediately knew it was Adam. He had a habit of calling and saying, "It's me" without leaving his name. Though it was a bit pretentious for him to think he would be the only "me" calling, I found it somewhat amusing. I wrote out his number and decided to wait a day to call him. I had started taking surfing lessons and had a lesson to go to anyway. The next day, I called him from work, during a break for coffee. The phone rang three times.

"Hello?"

"Hi, Adam. It's me, Libby."

"Hey, Libby, Libbs, it's great to hear your voice. How's it going?"

"Yeah, life is great! I'm in San Diego, and it appears you are, too, so what's going on?"

"Well, I live here now. I decided to get my master's in bioinformatics and systems biology."

"Wow! That sounds heavy."

"Yeah, I'll be starting at UCSD in the fall. We should catch up over dinner and drinks. What do you say?"

"Yeah, sure, sounds exciting, I want to hear all about your travels and your decision to get your master's. When do you want to meet?"

"How about tonight? Do you have plans?"

"Yeah, uh, I do have plans, but I should be finished around seven. How about meeting around eight-ish?"

"Okay, eight-ish? That's perfect. How about I pick you up? Your dad gave me your address, so I know where you live."

"Ah, yeah, of course he did. Sure, no problem."

"You haven't told your family we aren't together, have you?"

"No, not yet."

"Yeah, me either. I didn't know how to say it."

"Yup, I know what you mean. Well, hey, I have to get back to work. See you tonight?"

"Sure, see you tonight. I've missed you, Libbs."

I paused before saying, "Yeah, it's been a while. Talk to you later, Adam."

It was evident Adam was cheerful and excited about talking with me, and it was great to hear his voice, but my heart was still bruised from the summer before, which made me anxious about seeing him in person.

17

SEEING ADAM AGAIN WAS GREAT. It was as if nothing had changed between us, no breakup, no distance in time or place. The only noticeable difference was Adam had cut his long blond hair into what I would describe as the all-American boy haircut. We gave each other a big hug, and we stayed in that position for a few minutes. Whatever nervousness I was feeling before fell away.

"I've missed you, Libby. You feel like home to me."

"You smell good. Let's enjoy this moment, okay? No words."

Gone was the smell of pachouli, and in its place were the smells of lemon and sandalwood. He hugged me tighter, and when he let go, we looked at each other, smiled, and then he kissed me. I didn't stop him. I enjoyed that kiss as much as I had the very first one. When colors and appendage locations started running through my mind, I broke away.

"Ah, what are we doing? Let me show you the pad, and then let's go grab some dinner. I am so hungry."

We chuckled. Our fingers still laced together, I led Adam through each room in the condo and showed him around.

"Wow, this is really nice, Libby."

"Yeah, my parents own it. I get to live here, rent free. It's exactly twenty steps to the beach, too."

"Cool. Do you need a roommate?"

"Maybe. Who's asking?"

We smiled at each other and giggled. Then we drove up the Pacific Coast Highway past Bird Rock to La Jolla and ate at Wahoo's Fish Taco. Adam enjoyed the wet burrito, and I had the chicken tortilla soup sans tortilla strips, a side of rice and two ounces of grilled chicken and mixed it all together. It was the most delish. We indulged in crazy stories over food and cervezas while sharing our adventures during the time we had been separated. We ate, we laughed and before returning to my place, Adam stopped to grab a six-pack of Pacifico, which was what we had been drinking at Wahoo's.

Once we got to my place, I grabbed a beach blanket; Adam popped open two beers, poured them into melamine cups; and together we walked the fun twenty steps to the beach, where we decided we should continue catching up. It was a beautiful night; with the sounds of waves crashing onto the sand and receding back over the rocks, the silence of everything else, the few stars we were able to see, it was all magical. After a few moments of breathing all of this in, Adam and I looked at each other and smiled. He took my beer and burrowed our cups into the sand. He took his fingers and gently moved my hair away from my face, cupping my cheeks as he pulled me toward him, and we began kissing again.

Pulling away after becoming entranced by the kiss, I picked up my beer and took a sip.

"Adam, what are you doing with me? Why did you call, and why are you kissing me?"

"I'm sorry, Libby. I know what I said in Flagstaff, but every time I try to tell my family and friends we are no longer together, I can't. Like, it won't come out of my mouth. I've tried getting over you, so many times, with other women while in South America, but you . . . *you!* You are the one I think about when I lie in bed at night and when I wake up in the morning. Regardless of where I am, I can only see you in my mind's eye, and when you aren't there, it's heartbreaking. While I was backpacking in Patagonia I looked up, saw the most beautiful vista and thought to myself, 'If only Liberty were here, this would be perfect.' I realized during that trip just how much I love you. You are my best friend, and I don't want a life without you in it. Will you please give me a second chance?"

I looked out to the ocean, taking in the magical moment, allowing the whisper of the waves to tell me the way. I turned to Adam and looked him in the eye to see if there was anything I wasn't hearing, anything he wasn't saying. I lifted my cup as if to toast, and Adam followed suit.

"To second chances, Adam. Do not fuck me over!"

"I won't, Libby, I promise! To second chances!"

We touched our melamine cups together, finished off our drinks and sealed the deal with a kiss. Somehow, from out of nowhere, I heard someone call out, "Left hand, yellow circle." Of course, the words were in my head, and just like that, Adam and I were back together again.

18

DURING THE REMAINDER of that summer, Adam and I took in everything San Diego had to offer. Adam bought a surfboard, and we started surfing together. We also took up sailing in the San Diego Bay, which soon became my favorite thing to do. Seriously, who wouldn't love being barefoot on a boat powered by the wind, where you can hold on to a lifeline, close your eyes and feel like you are flying, where the salt air graces your skin while the warmth of the sun relaxes your senses. The best part was folding in the sails and setting anchor, letting the ocean sway and rock us gently while we were watching the sunset, my favorite way to close the day.

Closing my eyes now, I can imagine the sway that brings me peace. The thought makes my soul whisper "namaste," a simple greeting to beautiful Mother Earth from the core of my aching soul. I loved sailing so much I took the required classes to become a certified sailor and attempted to set sail as often as I could, sometimes daily.

We watched outdoor movies at Balboa Park; we experienced every beach San Diego had to offer and went to every zoo and theme park in the vicinity. At times, we ventured south into Baja and enjoyed its beaches and culture. We also ventured north into Orange County, LA, Catalina Island and Santa Barbara. In the winter, it was camping and hiking the Anza-Borrego Desert to Mariposa Palms or to the old railroad trestle.

In those days, we found ourselves becoming deeply committed to each other, unlike in any other attempt before. It was perfect. When it was time for school to begin, Adam moved in with me. He focused on his education and I on my career. During breaks, we would travel deeper into California to camp or hike and, in the winter, camp out and explore the desert. My parents came out to visit us often, and when Adam was locked into studies, my parents and I would make an escape to Coronado and spend the day sailing.

After a year, I decided to return to school myself to get my master's. It took awhile, working full time while going to school, but I earned both an MBA and a master's degree in Pacific international affairs. Adam's and my new schedules didn't really allow for either of us to do much of anything else, other than live the mellow life that surfing, sailing and camping around Southern California provided over the weekends when we were not consumed with studying. After Adam graduated, he contemplated going further to getting his PhD, but opted out as the cost of student loans was starting to weigh on him. He sought and landed an awesome opportunity with a local pharmaceutical company. I was so proud of him. We celebrated his milestone with two weeks in South America, where he showed me a few of his favorite backpacking locations. South America is majestic. Bogotá and Medellín in Colombia, as well as Quito and the Mindo forest in Ecuador, reminded me of being in Southern California as the plants and colorful flowers were similar and the air temperature embodied that Pacific coolness. When I graduated, my parents surprised us with a two-week getaway to Bali, where we spent time surfing and partying with the locals. It was a spectacular trip that added luster to the adventurous life Adam and I were creating together.

Looking back now, I realize what my parents wanted for me. They wanted me to have an opportunity to see all walks of life, all the while maintaining their lessons of simplicity and family roots, my grounding. It was their desire for me to have real adventures around the world before settling down with children of my own; to learn, to understand and be able to teach real love. They wanted me to be able to discover just who Liberty Rose Anderson really was, to build my personal foundation on top of the solid grounding they had provided for me. After all this time, I now understand, at a deeper level, why my father was upset about my pregnancy when I was so young.

Had I not lost the child, I wonder where I would be. Would I be in San Diego working at the World Trade Center? Would I have my MBA and master's degree in Pacific international affairs? Would I even have my bachelor's? Would I be like so many other children whose parents had banked some serious cash and who were living off their parents' wealth, never making anything of myself? What would my accomplishments have been? Would my tombstone have read, "Liberty Rose Anderson, single mother, lived off her parents' dime and had no personal accomplishments?" Depressing to consider.

Adam and I were making real money now. We were living together, but because we were not married, we kept our money separate. Adam's money was going to pay his student loans and into savings, while mine was going to savings, travel, clothes and solitary moments at the spa. To give back, I contributed some funds into my family's trust, volunteered my time and made donations to causes I believed in, using the name of the family trust.

Adam and I were happy.

19

IT WAS THE WINTER OF 2004, a week before Christmas, when Adam and I rode the Amtrak up to Santa Barbara for the weekend, partly to Christmas shop, and mostly to enjoy Santa Barbara during this amazing time. It was cold. My hands were freezing. Adam and I walked into a cozy restaurant where I ordered a bowl of chicken posole and a cup of hot chocolate. We were sitting near the fire, but not close enough. My fingers were so cold they felt like they would break if bent.

"Are you all right, Libbs?"

"I don't know why I can't warm up my fingers. Hopefully that hot chocolate will come soon."

"Here, let me see them."

We were sitting directly next to each other. I moved my hands toward Adam. He reached out and held both of my hands cupped within his own, which were warm. As my hands started to warm up, my hot chocolate arrived. Like a moth to a flame, I quickly reached over and wrapped both hands around the hot cup and held it for several minutes.

"Thanks, Adam. My hands feel normal now."

Smiling, I reached over and kissed his cheek. He smiled in return.

"Where are your gloves?"

"Um, I think I must have dropped them or something. I can't find them."

"That sucks."

We smiled and I took a sip of my hot cocoa.

"Hey, this may not make your hands feel warmer, but I've wanted to give this to you for a while."

I turned to look at Adam, curious.

"Yeah, what is it?"

He pulled my hands back into his, and at that moment, he put his mouth close to my ear and started to whisper.

"You know I love you, don't you?"

Chuckling, I replied using a whispered tone as well. "Maybe, Adam. I'm still trying to figure that out."

"You should know, Liberty. You should know in your heart, and mind, that I love you."

For a moment, I pulled back so our eyes could meet. Time seemed to stand still. Our faces drew closer and we softly kissed.

"I do, Adam. I know."

"Liberty Rose Anderson, will you make me a better man by becoming my wife? Will you please marry me?"

I tried to pull away so I could look at Adam's face, but he didn't let me move. He held my fingers firmly and pulled me in closer so our foreheads touched.

"I love you, Libby. What do you say?"

"Yes! Yes, Adam, I will marry you."

Tears streamed down my cheeks, and as I tried freeing my fingers to brush them away, Adam reached over and wiped them for me, and then kissed my cheek. He reached into his pocket and pulled out a small ring box. Inside was the most beautiful engagement ring, a single carat solitaire diamond on a white gold band. It was so simple, so perfect. Taking my hand, he leaned forward to kiss my ring finger and then slid the ring all the way down. It fit perfectly. I held my hand up to see the sparkle, the glimmer as the light refracted mini rainbows symbolizing a love to behold. I was enamored. Real joy emanated from deep within the well of my soul, and I felt as though my eyes were twinkling and delight was evident in my voice. I forgot about the cold. I was happy, incredibly so.

The rest of the night was filled with laughter and talk about how we would tell our parents. It was an exciting night for us both, and we were filled with giddy champagne-like exuberance.

20

FOR CHRISTMAS THAT YEAR, my parents hosted our traditional family get-together at their house in Colorado. Adam's family was invited, as were the Upchurchs. This would be the first time we included Adam's family in any of our festivities and the second time our parents had met. The first time was at our college graduation when they had met us for dinner.

It had snowed all Christmas week, which made the house look like a winter wonderland. Mr. Upchurch, Peter, decked out a horse with Christmasy garlands and a wagon with hay bales and a lot of blankets. One by one, we piled in and sat close to one another, if only to contain our body heat. With Peter and Mazy Upchurch at the helm, we were guided on a leisurely ride around the family lot with covered hot cups of rum apple cider in our hands. Adam's mother, Diane, began singing Christmas carols, and we all sang along.

Later that evening, we gathered in the living room drinking rum-spiked eggnog, talking, laughing and playing games. Adam pulled his father, and mine, toward him, showing four cigars. They, along with Peter Upchurch, went outside to smoke. As I was watching, I saw Adam exhale a few smoke rings, and as he relaxed, he said something. All three men looked at one another, at Adam and then at me. I smiled and waved with my right hand. I assumed Adam had shared our secret with them. They all hugged one another and shook hands. It was fun to watch.

"Hey, superstar, is everything all right?"

My mother was watching me watch the men outside. That night she wore a long flowing skirt of royal-blue velvet she had handmade for this occasion, and a loose silver cashmere sweater that rested low at her hips. It was layered with a loose scarf around her neck. She had handmade that, too. It was of the same royal-blue color, embroidered with small silver stars. Her hair was pulled back in a low ponytail bun and elegantly graced with three small shimmering crystal barrettes. She sparkled and looked beautiful.

"Yeah, I'm great, Mom, very happy. It's awesome to see Adam and Dad get along, that's all."

Leaning in to me, she hooked her right arm into my left, and together we took in the sight of the men we loved.

"Adam turned out to be an all right guy after all. I will admit, your father and I had our reservations."

"Mmm, yeah, I understand why. It has been a long, hard road with us. But, you both should know, we really love one another."

"Hmm, yes, I see that."

"Adam shows he loves me. It's not as sickening to watch as you and Dad, of course, but it is nice," I said jokingly and then leaned in to her shoulder.

My mother laughed and refilled our cups with fresh nog.

"You know," she said, "your father was my first true love. He has been my only love. He courted me in that old-fashioned kind of way, you know? He would come by early for our dates if only to talk with my mother and my father. He courted all of us, really, bringing fresh-cut flowers for my mom, Scotch or cigars for my dad. He was taught to be a gentleman during a time that type of man was being phased out. After a year, your father stopped by to ask my parents to lunch, without me. The motive was to present his case to ask me to marry him. Both my mother and father loved him and were more than happy to say yes. That next weekend, your father and I drove out to Yosemite, pitched a tent and hiked up a trail. Gosh, just thinking about it brings back all of these old feelings. I can still smell the freshness of the mountains. I remember your father packed a lunch in his backpack: wine, cheeses, fruits and peanut butter sandwiches. He rolled out his sleeping bag as a blanket; we sat, ate, and that is when he asked me to marry him. Ahhh, it was the best day, that day. One year later, we were married and my life has been wonderful ever since. We didn't dare move in together the way you and Adam did. Times are different now, I suppose. Are you really happy, darlin'?"

She reached up with her fingers and gracefully brushed my hair back behind my ears. Her eyes were wet with the tears that had welled up during her story.

"You are such a beautiful girl, with your father's eyes. You are a perfect combination of us both. We just want you to be happy."

Reaching up with my right hand, I held hers for a moment, pulled it toward my heart and said, "Yes, Mom, I am very happy. I'm not sure I've ever said this to you, but I am so grateful for the life you and Dad provided for me. I know how lucky I am."

I decided to tell my mom about the engagement, but at that point, my dad walked up and placed his arms around my mom and me. He had heard what I'd said.

"You're welcome, Libby. Your mom and I wouldn't have had it any other way. We are so proud of all you have accomplished and who you are becoming."

My mother nodded in agreement, and I hugged each of them. Adam came in and asked, "Hey, is this an Anderson family moment only?"

We all laughed and my father yelled out, "Champagne toasts by the fireplace; come gather around."

With that, my mother and I smiled, looked at each other, and as she slid her hand down my arm, onto my left hand, our fingers laced, and that was when she felt the ring. She pulled up my hand so she could see it, and then she turned to me with a stunned look and finally a smile. She hugged me and let out a little squeal.

"Mom! Shhh. Don't be so loud."

"Oh my God, Libby! Why didn't you tell me?"

"Well, I was looking for the perfect moment. It's been so busy, and really, there has been no private time between you and me, until now. I wanted to tell you after your story, but Dad walked up. Please, don't say anything, yet. Adam wants to announce it."

"Seriously, Liberty, this is a beautiful moment. I can't wait to hear the whole story."

"Thanks, Mom. I love you, you know."

She sighed and we followed everyone, led by my father, the pied piper of the day, into the living room with bottles of crispy cold champagne in our hands. My mother's excitement was clearly expressed across her face and in her walk.

"Come everyone. Fill your glass and let's get ready for a Christmas toast to remember!"

The fluted glasses were already set out, as this was an Anderson Christmas tradition. Everyone gathered around to pick a flute, my mother filling each glass with glee. My father loved life and looked for every opportunity to celebrate the little moments life had to offer. During Christmastime, it was usually the previous year he honored, and the promise of the upcoming year, and of course, his family that made it all worth living.

"This Christmas season is one I'd like to celebrate by first recognizing all of you fine people who are a crucial part of the Anderson family. Peter, Mazy, we love having you here. The kindness and peace the two of you radiate reminds us of how the choices we make in our lives matter, especially as we strive to attain a certain level of happiness. You two have been a part of our family for so long it would feel empty if you chose to celebrate Christmas elsewhere.

"Rich, Diane, if it weren't for Adam and Libby's relationship, we would not have had the privilege of getting to know you both. You are full of grace, and your warmth and generosity are welcomed with true gratitude. Welcome to our home, and to our Christmas celebration. Our family is bigger and richer than we ever dreamed possible, with you in it.

"Here in the Anderson household, we base our Christmas celebration on how successful our year has been according to the bounty of Sarah's garden, and all we have been able to harvest every season of this year. We started by planting a seed, which we nurtured throughout its growth cycle with caution and utmost care. In the spring, we watered, fertilized and prayed. During the summer, we continued to toil over the land to ensure all we had harvested was plentiful for our sustenance during the summer and fall, with the rest being preserved for our enjoyment during the winter, this winter. You may notice the delectables that have been set before you are from our garden and our farm. This year we have been blessed with filled cupboards, freezer and bellies.

"With all of you joining us this Christmas, our hearts and home are filled with abundant love. What can be better than that, eh? Without love, everything else is just what it is: food, water, house, absent of meaning. Sarah, Liberty and I can truly say, we want for nothing more. Let us drink a toast to our many blessings!"

We clinked flutes and took a drink in celebration. It was magical, with each clink resonating with a "ting" that added glimmer to our already bubbly Christmas bliss. Adam took my hand and pulled me in close for a Christmas kiss.

"I love you, Liberty Rose."

My parents, Adam's parents, Mazy and Peter, were enveloped with Christmas kisses and love, as well.

Adam then asked if he could give the next toast. My father took a deep breath, put my mother's hand in his and said yes. As we refilled our glasses, we all watched as Adam cleared his throat. It was obvious he was nervous.

"Karl, Sarah, thank you for welcoming my family, and me, into your beautiful home and into your hearts. Who knew, almost twelve years ago, we would all be in this home, at this moment, as one family coming together?"

Adam's father raised his glass and said, "Hear, hear." We all repeated the cheer, took a sip, and then Adam continued.

"Libby . . .Liberty and I have walked quite a path since we first met. I am sure you all had your concerns, but I am grateful you allowed Libby and me to make our own crazy choices without interfering. That means a lot. As you know, we have weathered the time and stress it took to get our bachelor's and our master's degrees so we can have healthy careers, so I am able to provide Liberty with a home as sound as the one she grew up in."

I looked at my parents, who had inched closer. My dad's arm was around my mom's shoulder, and she was leaning into him while holding her flute daintily. They smiled at Adam and gave nods of approval. I could see tears welling up in my mother's eyes.

"Liberty, what can I say? There is not a moment in life I do not see you in it. My time in South America felt like an eternity as I searched for you in places I knew I would never find you. With you, I know I am home. You are the beacon, the northern star to guide me home when I am lost, the sun in my dark sky and the light of my path. You are my direction forward. My life is empty without you in it. Liberty, will you make me a better man by becoming my wife?"

At that point, I looked around and I could see everyone was as happy as I was. I looked at Adam and responded, "Adam, I can't imagine myself anywhere else than beside you as your wife. Hell yeah!"

We all raised our glasses, cheered, sipped champagne, and for the rest of that night, that week, life was perfect.

21

THE ENGAGEMENT REPLAYS continuously in my mind. The engagement in Santa Barbara, the engagement in my family's home where everyone laid witness, the happiness we felt—all of it, over and over. I cannot place where we went wrong.

How is it that, a little over a year later, Adam wants to call it quits? How is it that one year would be so life altering? Even as I sit here, on my thinking log, recounting our relationship from the time we reconnected in San Diego until now, I cannot see the catalyst. I can see many reasons why we should have stayed apart before, why I should have said, "Fuck you, Adam, and your flaky, noncommittal ways. I'm looking for someone better."

But, I didn't.

After the engagement announcement in Colorado, we went back to San Diego and officially started to tell our coworkers and close friends. There were so many small parties, and of course, my parents were at all of them. My life was my parents' life, and vice versa. They wanted to know and be a part of everything, especially for this momentous milestone. This milestone was theirs, too.

Adam and I started to look for a house. At times, we contemplated having a new house custom built for us. My parents and his parents said they would each give a lump sum as a down payment when we found what we were looking for. Over the past several years, our savings accounts had become pretty healthy, and we would both be able to match our parents' gifts, and a little more, making our down payment that much bigger. We were excited.

During the month of June, Adam was nose down on a project. We pushed out the actual wedding date six months to accommodate his project deadline, meaning we would get married during the next summer, 2006, which was another year away. I was okay with that. It just seemed normal. Considering we hadn't been in a rush to get engaged, a delayed wedding just seemed, well, appropriate.

Over the next six months, as Adam poured his soul into his project, I worked with my mom on planning the wedding, as well as being consumed myself with my job responsibilities. My hard work paid off, because sometime in this period, I was called into my direct manager's office.

"Liberty, hey, come in. Sit down."

"Hey, Tom, thanks! What's going on?"

"Well, I want you to know, we have noticed all of your good work here in the office and thought that we could reward you, if you're interested, with a new role."

"Really? Doing what?"

"Well, the Asia Desk is looking for a replacement for Gerry. As you know, she will be taking a role within another department here at the World Trade Center. Your role would be director in trade missions, working under Sandy Newberry. You know him, right?"

"Yeah, I know Sandy, great guy."

"If you're interested in learning more, Sandy is interested in talking with you. You just have to say the word."

"Wow! That's big. I know what Gerry was up to; we talked about some of her projects quite a bit."

"Yeah, she is the one who recommended you in the first place, said you had some great ideas. You should talk to Sandy, get more details about the job. If you're into it, then let me know. If you're not, no problem, you can stay here with me."

"No, yeah, I'm interested. Sign me up. Let me know when Sandy's available, and I'll meet up with him."

"Perfect! He's available tomorrow at 2:00 p.m. Meet at his office."

"Great! Thank you, Tom. I'll be there."

After meeting with Sandy, I got the job and started to travel to Japan, China and Taiwan, which meant I didn't see Adam as often, and the wedding would be pushed out to Christmas of 2006.

22

WITH OUR NEW CHRISTMAS TRADITION locked in from the time of the engagement announcement, Adam, his family and I went to my parents' house for Christmas the next year. It was more of the same as the year before, except this year, Adam seemed distant, withdrawn. My assumption was his project was wearing him down. Once we got home, things seemed all right. In March 2006, everything changed.

"Hey, Libby."

"Hey, Adam."

"Will you go for a walk on the beach with me? Let's get out of here for a while."

"Yeah, okay, let me grab my sweater."

It was a beautiful day. The sun was shining, the sea gulls were calling out, the sky was brilliantly blue and there were many beach lovers enjoying the comforting power of the ocean. The coolness of the Pacific enveloped us all as the sounds of the ocean waves crashing onto the beach reminded us that we were all intricate particles of this beautiful earth. Adam wove his fingers in mine.

"Libby, I don't know how to tell you this, but I found out some horrific news last week. By law, I have to share it with you."

"This sounds like I should have my right hand on a Bible, sitting down, or something. So ominous."

"Mmm, yeah, uh, maybe we should sit down. Um, how about over here?"

We walked to a secluded section of the beach and sat down. Adam looked out and grew quiet. I followed his gaze and saw nothing but the horizon. As I looked back at him, he appeared more pensive.

"So, what is it, Adam? Trepidation is building."

He looked back at me and just stared into my eyes with a look of pained uncertainty.

"Um, I don't know how else to say this Libby, except to come out and say it. It's going to be harsh, but I need you to be mature about your reaction, okay?"

"All right, I will try, Adam, but enough with the histrionics. I'm dying here."

Adam paused before finally saying, "Libby, I've been diagnosed with the AIDS virus."

"What the fuck? Adam!"

"Libby, give me a chance! Let me talk to you."

"Yeah, okay, sorry, this is just so unexpected. Please, go ahead."

"A few months ago, this girl, someone I knew from my past, found me and gave me the news she had AIDS and I should get tested. So, I finally did. The results came in last week and they were positive."

"What? Adam, let me see the results. Where are they?"

"It's not like I carry them around like a badge of honor, Libby. I just—I don't have them on me. I was so upset, I burned the results."

"Oh my God, Adam! Why in the hell would you burn the results?"

I stood, folded my arms and stared out to the ocean. My mind was reeling with the steady pace of the surf, the crashing waves, one after another, the surf hitting the sand, and the waters receding, building again and continuing this flow. The reality of this ridiculous notion, that Adam had AIDS, jabbed deeper into the freshly reopened wound from my previous heartbreaks with Adam. My tears began streaming down previously burned cheeks. With sincere curiosity, I restated the question.

"This isn't small news you are giving me here, Adam. Why in the hell would you burn the results, and why didn't you tell me about this when you first learned of it? I could have taken the test with you. I could know, right now, if I had it as well. Oh my God, what are we going to do?"

This news was unfathomable, and while our relationship was questionable, for the first time since the baby sitch, the question of my future was uncertain.

"I don't know, Liberty! I just didn't."

"Well, what do we need to do? What is your doctor saying?"

"He's referred me to a specialist. My appointment is next week. I think we should call off the wedding, don't you? I've been thinking about it, and I think I should move out."

"What? What the . . .Adam, look at me. What are you talking about?"

"Liberty, fucking look at *me*! I am a man with AIDS, a walking dead man! How in the hell am I going to support you now? I can't, Libby. I just can't! You deserve much better."

Adam began to cry, and I sat down next to him wondering how all of this had happened. I wrapped my arm around his arm and rested my head on his shoulder. All the while staring, blankly, out to the ocean, watching as the setting sun seemingly dimmed the light of my future of being a wife or a mom, as each moment slowly faded to black.

Who was the girl who had given him this news? It could have been the Louisiana girl, Mandi, the girl from the bathroom. Hell, it could have been anyone. How had she explained this fucked up situation to Adam? I felt numb. With the sound of the receding waves moving back into the beautiful Pacific Ocean, the painful ooze of this reopened wound flowed as burning hot tears down my cheek.

"Libby, if I have it, you probably do, too. You need to get yourself checked. If you don't have it, then you should move on. I won't want you to take care of me. I won't let you. I don't deserve it."

Adam's voice was a hollow whisper, vacant, deep, flat. In my head, it pinged like an echo from a sea gull calling in the distance. The faint sound of his voice revived me from my stupor.

"What? Adam, don't be silly. It's for better or for worse; in sickness and in health, remember? Marriage vows."

My voice, also a hollow whisper. Of course, this was not how I'd expected our married life to begin. We had talked about traveling a bit more, getting all of those wants out of our system so we could start our own family. This news changed everything.

"So, who is the girl, Adam?"

"You don't know her, Libbs. It doesn't matter, anyway."

With that, Adam got up. I didn't look up; rather, I stayed seated and told him I needed a moment.

"It's getting cold. Ready to go back?"

"Go ahead. I'll be in shortly. I just need a few more minutes."

He walked away, toward home, and I sat there watching each wave pummel the sand. Hoping, with each crash, I would wake up from this nightmare, or the waves would flow over me and wash this dirty news off of me. I closed my eyes for a few moments and started to cry.

I cried for a while.

23

I STAYED BEHIND UNTIL THE SUN had set, and even then, I had to force myself to stand up and go forward. As I moved around, I realized how cold I really was. I walked home as quickly as possible. When I got there, Adam was gone. Because I was so cold, I walked straight into the bathroom, undressed and jumped into a tolerably hot shower in the hope of warming up my cold soul, as well as washing the mucky AIDS news off of me. I stood, facing the spray, as the hot water streamed down my face, around each strand of hair on my head, all the way to my toes, allowing my hot tears to be combined with the hot water from the shower head. How would I give my parents this news? This would not be a milestone to be celebrated with crisp champagne toasts and laughter.

After a while, the water started to cool. I turned it off, dried myself and wrapped myself in my cozy robe. Standing there for a few minutes, I used the robe as my blanket and wrapped it around myself even more tightly, to maintain the warmth. I stopped at the mirror to put on some facial cream. My eyes were red, and I quickly looked away and left the bathroom. Adam still wasn't home. I went into the kitchen to open up a bottle of red zin, my liquid remedy of this moment, and there, tucked beneath the bottle, was a note from Adam.

"Liberty Rose, I am sorry I brought hell into your heart . . . into your home. I love you, but I can't be here right now. –A."

I went to the bedroom as I simply wanted to get under the bed-covers, hoping I could fold my self inward for solace. The closet door was open. Going over to close it, I realized his clothes and shoes were gone. I checked his drawers: empty. I went into the bathroom: everything, gone. I couldn't believe it. I called his cell phone, but it rang until it went to voice mail. I did this again, and again, for the rest of the night. Regardless, I got the same result until the last call went straight to voice mail. Either Adam had turned off his cell, or the battery had died. I didn't know which, and it didn't matter. He simply wasn't taking my calls.

The next day, I called in sick, and then I called Adam's office. No answer. Then I called his assistant and, unfortunately, had to tell a small fib.

"Hi, Lisa, it's me, Libby."

"Hi, Libby, are you looking for Adam?"

"Yeah, uh, we are supposed to meet later. I forgot where."

"Oh, well, Adam took a few weeks off. He said you and he would be going camping. I thought you two were leaving this morning?"

"Ah, yeah, late start. He said he needed to pick something up. I thought he meant from the office; maybe he meant the storage unit. No worries, Lisa, we'll catch up. Thanks."

"All right, Libby. Have a great time."

"Thanks, Lisa. Good-bye."

That afternoon, I went to the office of Dr. Hannah Whiteman, my doctor, and asked for a visit. I mentioned I would be willing to wait all afternoon, if I had to. I was not leaving without being tested.

After an hour of waiting, I was called into her office where I sat and dished out my entire sob story about how I thought I had AIDS, about how Adam, my fiancé, had it and about how I didn't know what that would mean for my quality of life.

"So, let me make sure I understand. Adam is saying he actually has AIDS?"

"Yes. He said he tested positive and if he has it, I probably do, too."

"Hmm. Has he been sick lately?"

"No, not really."

"Have you?"

"Um, not really. I mean, sometimes I get the sniffles, but only after surfing. It goes away, but I wouldn't say I've been sick."

"Liberty, tell me, how much do you know about AIDS or even HIV?"

"Aargh, I'm embarrassed to say, Doc, I should know more about it. On the periphery, I know infection only occurs when blood transfer occurs; so if I have AIDS and I cut myself and bleed, if you help me and you have an open wound of some sort, say a paper cut, and my blood enters your wound, then transfer could occur. Kissing or touch does not transfer the virus. I know a mother can transfer the disease to her unborn child. I know a lot of people have died because of AIDS, and not in a remotely decent way. What I'm also aware of is it's transmitted sexually, anyone can get it and there is not a cure, yet."

For the first time in a while, I felt like the most undereducated person in the room. How was it I did not know anything more recent about a disease affecting so many people? So many people who had been diagnosed, in or out of my community, and had lived with the disease until it killed them. So many people, whose loved ones will never be the same with the loss of one more who fell victim to this wretched disease. Because of what I did know about the disease, I was in a manic state of uncertainty.

"All right, that's fair," she said. "Between you and me, not many people know as much as they should about something that can change a person's quality of life so quickly and so drastically. On the periphery, you seem to have a good understanding of how one might experience the transfer, and how to potentially avoid it. The first thing we should be clear on, Libby, is AIDS and HIV are related but should not be confused as being one and the same.

"HIV is an acronym for human immunodeficiency virus, which is a virus only affecting humans. This virus attacks the immune system, which causes that system to be deficient. A person who becomes infected with HIV can become infected with AIDS over time. That's somewhat distressing to consider, I know, but the AIDS infection takes anywhere from eight to ten years, after a person has been infected, to happen. HIV is the first thing to happen.

"So, AIDS is an acquired immunodeficiency syndrome. It's an 'acquired' disease because a person has acquired the HIV infection. 'Immunodeficiency' because a person has symptoms of a weakened immune system, meaning your body is unable to fight off diseases. This happens next, but many years later. It is important to know, there are no symptoms. The only way to know is to get tested.

"Most people think this is a gay man's disease. While it is true that in some parts of the world AIDS took hold in the gay man's community, what is key to know is that in other parts of the world, HIV is prevalent in heterosexual couples. Almost half of the people infected are women. At the end of the day, Liberty, you are right: it is most definitely a sexually transmitted disease. You are also correct: as of today, there is no cure. That's pretty harsh, I know, so before I move on, thoughts? Questions?"

Every word Dr. Whiteman said was weighted with a level of heavy I was struggling to fathom. It was clear an immunodeficiency meant real sickness; that was not really my struggle. My angst was with Adam. How the hell did he not know this? Why wouldn't he have just let me know when he found out? With Adam not talking to me now, the real question was, did I have it, and what would be my quality of life, if I did?

"Yes, Doc, thanks for letting me know. On a serious note, I have to ask myself how I, an educated woman who loves to learn and read everything, do not know as much I should about how the impact of this disease has grown. You are saying almost half of those infected are women? It sounds like anyone could have HIV and not even know it. Shouldn't there be more awareness about it?"

"That's right, Liberty. HIV does not exhibit real symptoms for years. HIV/AIDS is a pandemic, meaning this sickness is a global crisis, not one to ignore or to be swept under the rug. A lot of beautiful people are infected daily. Some don't even know they have the infection, which is unfortunate, because they go on infecting other people, thereby spreading the disease, hence the pandemic. According to AIDS.gov, in the US alone, there are more than 1.2 million people living with the HIV infection, and worse, one in eight of those infected are not even aware they have it. Those statistics are from my last visit to that website. I strongly recommend you hit up that site when you go home. There is a lot of great information there, very helpful information.

"While this is devastating to you now, you should walk away knowing Adam has done you a favor; at least you can get yourself tested, learn more about it and change your lifestyle accordingly. In my opinion, everyone should be tested if they have had sex with even one partner, because you just don't know if that person has had unprotected sex with someone infected with the virus. We could eradicate this disease if everyone took a moment to learn more about it and took the responsibility to be more cognizant of how their actions impact others."

Dr. Whiteman looked at me with a warm smile. It was clear she was trying to reassure me. Then she sat next to me, placed her hand on my shoulder and squeezed it.

"All right, I'll get off of my soapbox now."

I smiled, but at this point I could not laugh at her attempt to be a little funny.

"Yeah, I see. So, what are the symptoms I need to be aware of? If I have it, how will my quality of life be going forward? Will I be able to work? Will I be able to go on long backcountry camping excursions? I still don't know what any of this means for me."

"Well, there is a lot to learn, such as, there are no symptoms for HIV. This is very important to remember. Look, the first thing, Liberty, is to not panic. Let's see if you really have the HIV virus or not."

Dr. Whiteman explained what it would mean to be HIV positive and how my life would change going forward. Essentially, if I was infected, my world would consist of a permanent, daily drug treatment. Aside from my inconsistent 420 moments, I do not enjoy any other drugs. I can't even remember to take a daily vitamin. My preference is for health and wellness from eating clean and exercising regularly. (Sigh.) It didn't matter how she put it; nothing she said was what I wanted to hear.

"Before we fret, let's take some blood work, and we'll send it in for testing, okay? Do you think you might be pregnant, Libby?"

The question took me by surprise, as the idea of being pregnant had not dawned on me. It's not like we were being careful, but while we had discussed the thought of getting pregnant, it was with the plan of doing so — later.

"Pregnant? No. Of course it's always possible, but I don't think so. I mean, we weren't trying, but we weren't not trying either."

"All right, well, in the meantime, I am going to give you a prescription for Xanax to help you relax. I should have the results in the next day or so. Would you like me to call you at home or work?"

"No, will you please call me on my cell? If I don't pick up, will you please leave a message?"

"Sure, is that number in your file?"

"Yes, it should be."

As she checked my file for my contact details, I admitted that my attempt to absorb this info was overwhelming.

"Do you have a support group you can lean on, Liberty? That's important. If your lab work does come back positive, you are really going to need a stable support system."

"My parents are pretty amazing. They live in Colorado. Actually, I am planning to fly out there in the morning to talk with them about this newfound situation of mine."

"That's great, Liberty."

Dr. Whiteman smiled and handed the prescription to me. I stared at the chicken scratch without trying to decipher what each line meant. At that point, I simply didn't care. I just wanted to know whether I had the fucking virus or not.

"Here is my card," she said. "If you have additional questions or if you do not hear from me in a couple of days, please do not hesitate to call."

"Actually, I don't know anything about Xanax, as I don't usually take prescription meds. Will you please prescribe a low dose of Valium instead? I probably won't take it, but at least it is a drug I have heard of and used once before."

"Sure, Liberty."

"Thank you, Dr. Whiteman. I appreciate how kind you've been to me, and mostly, thanks for seeing me without an appointment."

With a somber smile, I waved to her as she left the room with my chart, and she smiled in return. Her assistant came in and led me to the table where she would retrieve the possibly tainted blood from my veins. After the bloodletting was completed, I called my office and took the next week off. I mentioned I would be going to Colorado for a family emergency. Then I went online and bought the first ticket out of San Diego to Telluride.

24

"MOM, DAD, HELLO? Is anybody home?"

There was no answer. The door was unlocked as usual. The only people who came to the house anyway were people who lived here or were invited. I took my bag upstairs to unpack. Being in the room where I had grown up flooded my mind with memories. All of my favorite things covered the walls and all available counter space was filled with pictures from days gone by with friends, family, with Adam. Hanging on the hook of my closet door was my wedding dress. It was still beautiful, still waiting for my wedding.

Tears started to well up in my eyes, and I left the room with my bag untouched, zipped and fully packed. I decided to take a walk, but before I did, I went to my mother's desk, took out a note card and pen and jotted down a quick note to my parents.

"Hey there! It's me, Libby. I'm here for the week. That's my rental car in the drive. Went to the Thinking Log. Be back soon. xx"

I signed my name, Liberty Rose, and stood the note up on the kitchen counter where it would immediately be seen; then I followed the path to the creek and into the grove of trees to my favorite place to think about things. I called it the "Thinking Log."

I had been about ten years old when I first discovered it. I was sitting on a log from a tree previously cut down for firewood. That was my first thinking log. From there, I noticed an oak tree that appeared to have a better vantage point and, after a while, found the courage to climb her. It became my favorite place to go when my mother sent me out to explore the beauty of our land. When I returned, she would say, "Tell me about your adventures, Liberty, darlin'. I want to hear all about them."

Every story started with one simple sentence: "I went to the Thinking Log today, and you won't believe what I saw." She and my dad would sit and listen to the fantastical stories I would reel off, and then we would all laugh, together.

The Thinking Log is what I called this old oak tree, which quickly replaced the log on the ground. I would climb up and sit within the arms of the tree, sing songs, and gaze at everything around me, thinking, daydreaming about what could be. Over time, this little oak tree grew taller, as did I. The taller it grew, the wider the arms of the tree grew; the higher I climbed, the better my vantage point. Without having to turn my head, I could see the entire northern half of our property, as well as the path and our family home. I could even see where my mother or my father, sometimes both, had followed me outside. They were always a safe distance away in the event I needed their help, which I never had.

Today, however, they were not in their usual places. They weren't even in their home. They were nowhere to be found. They didn't know I was here, nor were they expecting me to be. It was just me, sitting in the tree, thinking about my life and all it meant.

25

THINKING BACK ON THAT NIGHT, years back when I was pregnant, when I went to Estes Park to contemplate my life as a single mother, I remember imagining the baby might have been a girl. After considering a lot of names, I settled on Samsara Jade, which essentially means "cycle of life," because we would become a cycle of life as mother and daughter. After losing the baby, knowing for certain it would have been a girl, I confided in Diane, Adam's mother, and confessed I had named the baby. Adam's sister was pregnant around that time, and guess what she named her child? Yup, Samsara Jade. I was appalled they would take my dead baby's name. I am appalled still, albeit somewhat curious about whether a Samsara Jade was meant to be born at that time. Both Adam's mother and his sister denied knowing anything about the name. Diane swore she did not recall talking about it. However, what a weird coincidence that we would both randomly come up with the same rare name. From that point on, my confessionals were voiced only to God or to my parents, or they were contemplated here, where the whispering wind takes a secret, and it dissipates into the Rocky Mountain air.

Before Adam asked me to marry him, in Santa Barbara, he and I had started talking about having children. We were sailing the San Diego Bay. It was quieter than usual, but pleasant sailing nonetheless.

"Hey, Libby, do you remember losing the baby?"

"That's something I'll never forget, Adam. Why do you ask?"

"Well, are you still interested in being a mother?"

The idea of this, of getting pregnant, being a mom, excited me. The whole big picture of our future was taking shape, and my well of happiness filled even more deeply.

"Absolutely! Now that we have our degrees and our careers in order, I can totally see it happening. You?"

I remember smiling with the thought. I was hopeful.

"Yeah, sometimes I do. Sometimes it scares me; like, what if I'm not able to provide for her, or him?"

"Mmm, yeah, that's a lot of pressure, for sure, but, you know, we make great money separately, and together we are doing amazingly well. We can do this, Adam."

"What if it's born with a physical defect and one of us has to quit our job? I don't know if I can do it on my own."

"Well, I make great money now, and I have been saving since I have moved here. Besides, I have a trust fund. If worse comes to worst, I know my parents will be there for us."

"Libby, what I am trying to say is, I don't want our parents' help. If we are going to do this, then it has to be *us* doing it. This is important to me, Liberty, that we are simpatico on this relationship being just you and me."

"All right, Adam, I get it. But what if it comes out normal and everything is perfect?"

"Yeah, that would be great. Will you be able to handle not home-schooling her or him?"

"Good question. We can look at options when that time comes. For now, we need to turn. Let's come about."

Today, as I sit and contemplate, I realize the babe from a time once before may have been my only shot at being a mother. If the AIDS test results return positive, I will never be a mother, much less a wife. Considering Adam has bailed on me, what man in his right mind is going to want a sick woman? I am now officially tainted. What about my job? How will my career be impacted? Will they still want me? Will I even have the energy to deal with this disease and work?

Even with my peripheral knowledge and what Dr. Whiteman shared, I know as much now about the bottom line as I did when I saw the news announcement almost twenty years ago, that being, *anyone can get it, and there is no cure.* What I also know: technology has improved and living with this disease can be done. I start to regain my hope and decide that, regardless of the results, I will find a way to live a quality life, with or without Adam. With or, hopefully, without the AIDS virus. What a mess!

Adam, sweet, fucking Adam!

Adam and I started out as friends, before becoming the best of friends. Over time, we became a family. Looking back at the last thirteen years of my life with Adam, I can see where things went right, and where things went wrong. When things were right between us, we had a lot of fun. When things were wrong, it was that friendship, and love, that kept us in each other's lives. Was friendship or love enough, though? When does loving someone become toxic? When a toxic love leaves one person, or both, somewhat debilitated, how do we walk away? Do we use the word "love" to mask feelings of guilt, codependency or fear of not being loved at all?

Adam has always found a reason to leave me. Strangely, it has never been during the times of chaos, like during the pregnancy.

Rather, he would decide to leave when things were great between us, such as after our post-graduation trip and now, right before our plans for the wedding were finalized. It suddenly dawns on me: Adam wanted out right before he knew I was pregnant. Then I lost the baby, so he stayed with me out of guilt. Guilt was probably the only reason he invited me to Nevada and why he went with me on our summer backpacking trip. That was probably why he moved to San Diego to get his master's. He probably felt guilty about how he had left our relationship. Guilt love is toxic love, and while it may be love, it is not a healthy love because it limits relationship bonding and growth. It stifles happiness.

Toxic love makes a person become like a dog, tethered and trapped behind a fucking chain link fence. Where you can see the possibility of what is out there, and it taunts you, but you can't do anything but stay put. Trapped love is not the kind of love I dreamed of, nor can I imagine it to be the kind of love for anyone. I've just realized, when a person wants out, you should let them out and not make it so easy for them to return. Adam is right. We should call the marriage off, and we should end whatever this relationship has been.

After a full day of sitting on the Thinking Log, analyzing our relationship, trying to understand how and when we could have been infected, it is time for me to climb down and tell my parents a story. As with the stories from before, this one will start with a simple sentence: "I went to the Thinking Log today, and you won't believe what I saw."

The sun will be setting in about an hour, and it's starting to get cold. My parents should be home by now. I am not looking forward to telling this story because I know after I bare all, there will not be laughter; rather, there will be questions, cursing and crying, but together we will find a way to make this work. This is my foundation, my safe haven, and I feel secure.

As I start to climb down, my foot slips and I lose my grip on the tree, and though I try to grab hold of a peg, I can't. I want to cry out, but my voice goes silent as my body sucks in air, as if I were falling into deep water. I fall thirty feet and land flat on my back, hard, within nature's palm. The same palm that showed me the way to the serenity my parents' refuge offered, catches and cradles me now.

Looking up, I can see the beauty of the sun setting in the sky. The blue is becoming deeper, with accents of reddish pink and orange slowly brushed in. It will be a matter of minutes before the sun sets completely. I try to call out, but the sound of my voice is only loud in my head. So, instead, I lie here, silently, paralyzed, attempting to use telepathy to call out to my dad, mom, Peter, Mazy—anyone who can hear my silent cries for help. It doesn't work. All I can do is continue gazing up. I can see the Thinking Log. This is the first time I've had a chance to view the simplicity of it from the ground. It is beautiful, private, unreachable from this point. My very own private haven. As I embrace my newfound vantage point, realizations start to set in. The most disturbing being, I have spent my entire adult life with a man I loved with all of my heart, with a man who did not love me in the same way.

Who knew, on that day of our first date, the number thirteen would mark the number of years we would spend together or even how many more years I would spend alive? When Adam told me he had the AIDS virus and I might have it also, my whole foundation was jolted. Everything I had lived for would shift into a new form, eroding who I had become up to that day, changing who I was forever. All I believed was now questioned, my life with Adam, his love for me.

In this, my last twilight, I finally realize Adam has spent thirteen years with a woman he loved but had no intention of marrying, even as much as he tried to do the right thing. It is clear, over time that he became complacent and out of guilt fulfilled his obligation until he just couldn't anymore. Adam held on to our relationship because he felt he would hurt me if he walked away, because of the baby we lost and his guilt about it. And now, I am dying.

I am dying because my mind has been so focused on the tragedy this wretched virus brought into my life that I missed my footing on the peg. I slipped and I couldn't pull myself together quickly enough. I fell thirty feet.

It's amusing, the things that come to mind right before the final fade-out from life. In this moment of my free fall, my first thoughts are, "Shit!" or "Wait! I can't move, or talk" and "How in the hell did that just happen?" Suddenly, memories, the kind sworn to be taken to the grave, replay in my mind's eye. It is usually during my 420 moments that I release all conflicting energy causing me heartbreak. It is when I come back here, to the Thinking Log, that I allow myself to step into the memory of that time, much like now, to remember that beautiful child I lost, the child whose gentle, gracious and amazing soul I humbly returned to God.

It's as though all of my past thoughts, once released with an exhale, reenter, as if only the hollow confines of nature know my innermost secrets. It is fitting that the moment to reflect is during my last breaths, cradled within the heart of Mother Earth. Tears flow down my cheeks, but I can't reach up to wipe them. In these last moments, my mind escapes to that time when I was almost a mother. Truly, there was no way I could bring a child into that emotional turmoil, resentment and anger. Samsara deserved better. I loved that baby more than anything I have ever loved. Yes, I made a conscious choice to abort the child. She would have been twelve this year.

It was not an easy decision. I spent weeks visiting different clinics, interviewing doctors, reading pamphlets, pleading to God and begging this tender soul, feeding from the sacredness of my innermost being, for forgiveness. The clinics were dirty, and after I had been to several of them, I excused myself and drove to a nearby bar. Sitting there, at a corner table in that darkened room, I ordered a glass of water and allowed the tears to slowly hug my cheeks. "What am I going to do?" was all I kept thinking. I pulled out my list of local abortion clinics. There was one more clinic remaining to be visited. In that moment, I decided if the last doctor's office and staff were acceptable, I would proceed with the deed. If not, then I would keep the child. This last place was my personal line in the sand, so to speak, a coin toss.

26

THE LAST PLACE, while somewhat shoddy, was the most respectable of them all. The entrance was discreet, and the building appeared to have been an old child day-care facility. The exterior was masked by a fading mural of happy children running and playing under a disappearing blue sky, like spirits that did not quite make it into this world. The interior had old-looking, but clean, carpet. The lady behind the glass window spoke with a warm kindness that had been severely lacking from the previous places I had seen. After I had disclosed the purpose of the visit, she gently asked me to relax in the waiting room. When I turned, there were cushioned recycled chairs, from decades before. On the wall nearest the restrooms were pockets of pamphlets discussing the procedure, as well as pamphlets for alternative measures, like adoption.

Piano solos were playing softly over the speaker. The place was calming, which helped me to relax a little. The doctor came out and sat next to me. I was the only one in the waiting room with him. He asked me several questions like: Are you okay? Are you sure this is what you want? Do you feel pressured or forced to do this? Are you alone? Do you have questions? We talked for at least twenty minutes. He then placed his hand on my shoulder, smiled and excused himself. There was nothing pretentious or shaming about this clinic. After a few minutes of his leaving me, I got up and made an appointment for that afternoon.

The light in the clinic's abortion room was dim, which helped me maintain a sense of composure. The nurse came in, provided me with a dose of valium and water. She never looked me in the eye, but her voice was soft, and her way was gentle. She gave me a hospital gown and asked me to change my clothes and lie back on the table, which was covered with crisp white paper, and told me to relax. She left, and I did as directed. I noticed the room was cold, and I put my sweater on, wrapping it around me as tightly as I could, like it was a blanket, and breathed in deeply. The doctor entered and gave me an ultrasound. I closed my eyes and focused on anything other than the moment, blocking out noises and voices until the doctor casually said, "Well, in case you are curious, it's a girl."

When he announced the gender, it was as if something registered. All I had considered was confirmed; it was a girl. I blinked a few times, and immediately, I recanted my decision.

"No! *Stop!* I can't! I won't do this. Please, stop!"

The doctor and nurse turned to look at each other and then at me. A level of frantic desperation washed over their faces. It made me more anxious, and I tried to get up.

"Please stop!"

"Uh, we can't! We have already injected the saline solution. I am sorry, but it is too late. She'll be permanently deformed," the doctor said with urgent exasperation. He then looked at the nurse pleadingly.

The nurse rushed to my side to get me to lie back down. At that moment, my soul lamented and I released a sound I cannot describe. My body collapsed into the hospital bed, convulsed, and I cried out loud. Whoever would have known this moment would be a milestone marker in my life? Certainly not I.

Giving this baby back to God was the most devastating act I have ever performed. It was at this moment I suddenly understood the story of the two women who approached King Solomon, each claiming, "I am this child's mother; make this woman give the child to me." In the story, King Solomon directs his guard to cut the child in half and give one half to each woman so they can each have what they both claimed belonged to them. One woman says, yes, cut the child. The real mother said, "No, please, do not cut the child in half. Give him to the other woman, so the child may live." King Solomon gave the child to her because he knew only the true mother would sacrifice her needs for that of her child, that she would rather give her lovely child to another so it would live. In my case, it was aborting my child to save her spirit and soul from being cut in half due to the neglect of her father, arguments between her father and mother over "her." That was my claiming, "I am the mother." My act of returning the soul of the child to God so another more deserving mother could have it would allow the angelic soul to live purely rather than suffering within a broken home.

After the abortion was complete, the nurse gave me a second valium and led me into a dark room where I could seek solace in private. The amount of valium wasn't enough. It might as well have been a placebo. I could not stop crying. I could not numb myself. Several minutes later she returned only to kick me out.

"Miss Anderson, I'm sorry, but you are going to have to leave. You are making the other young ladies feel uneasy. It is quite awkward. Surely you understand."

Slowly, I got up and dressed myself. There was a mirror, and I looked at the image of the woman who stood before me in the reflection. She was like a ghost; I didn't even know who that woman was, as she surely did not look like the "me" I knew, and loved, so well. To this day, that ghost remains captured in that mirror, because as I walked out of that building, it was as an empty shell to be filled anew. Two souls were aborted that day.

Life.

We are born into a mind and body, into a family, onto this beautiful earth we love and often take for granted. We love. Some may say we learn to love, but I believe we love the moment we make a connection with another soul. I am lucky to have known love, to have lived a great life.

If my death is to be like my life, happy and free, then I have to let go of any harbored feelings of anger or hate. With each remaining breath, I must accept everything encompassing who I have been, as Liberty Rose Anderson, with love, so when my spirit dissipates into the air you breathe, it is of love, so when you breathe in the air, the cycle of life continues with love. Samsara.

If only my parents were here.

My mind's eye is taking me back to a moment when, as a child, I am lying flat on a blanket, arms wide open, staring at the sky and creating images out of the billow of nimbus clouds rolling across. The sweet Rocky Mountain air is sweeping past my face, leaving cool-breeze kisses on my skin, tousling my hair. It's a beautiful, lazy spring day, and my parents are lying beside me. My mother's gentle melodic voice resonates softly, comfortingly, as she points to one cloud and then another, asking me, "Look, there, tell me, what do you see?" I hear the sound of my father's and my mother's chuckles when I respond. It feels real, as if they are really here, next to me, and we are crafting the stage before us out of bright, beautiful, fluffy clouds.

The sounds of their voices carry me home.

I take a deep breath, blink once and slowly let that breath out.

My last.

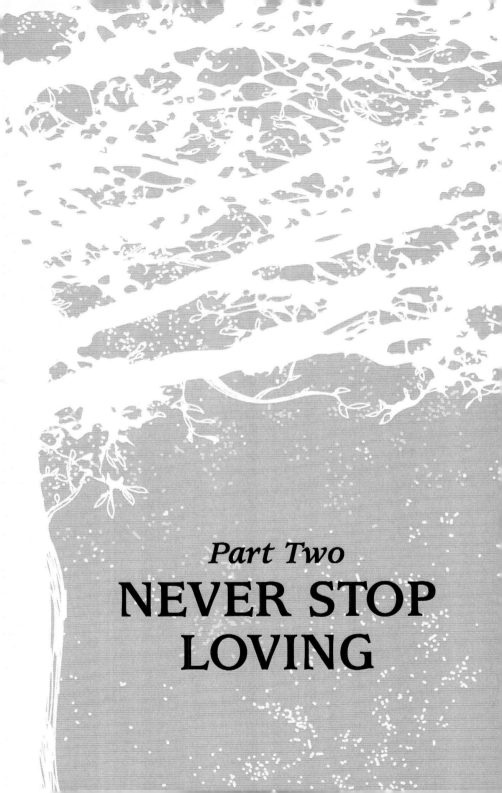

Part Two
NEVER STOP LOVING

27

"KARL, WHOSE CAR IS THAT?"

"I don't know, but I noticed it has Colorado plates. Let me call Upchurch and see if he knows anything about it."

"It's Peter Upchurch, leave a message and I'll call you back." Beep.

"Hmm, it went straight to voice mail."

"Leave a message, Karl, just in case something is wrong in there."

"Yeah, Peter, it's Karl. Hey, listen, there's a car parked out front, and I was wondering if you might have seen who pulled in. We are going into the house. Will you come by if you don't hear back from me in a few minutes? Thanks!

"Okay, Sarah, let's go in. Stay close to me, all right?"

"You know I will."

Karl flipped the lights on as he entered each room. There were no signs anyone had been there. When he and Sarah went into the kitchen, they saw a cell phone and a note sitting on the counter.

"Karl, that's Libby's cell phone. She must be here. How wonderful. I wonder if she has seen her wedding dress. I hung it upstairs."

Sarah excitedly ran to the stairs and called out to Liberty, but there was no answer.

"Libby, darlin', we're home! Come on down to see us."

She started to run up the stairs, but Karl called her back.

"Sarah, it appears Libby went for a walk. Let's start a fire and prepare something to eat. Knowing Libby, she'll be hungry."

"Great idea, Karl. You start the fire; I'll put on some music and start dinner. Oh, and call Peter. Let him know what's up."

"Deal."

Sarah put on a record by Nick Drake, one of her favorite music performers. She was convinced there was no better way to listen to music, other than on vinyl. She pulled out cheeses, homemade bread and crackers, as well as cut carrots and other treats from her garden, arranging everything neatly on a beautiful platter. She then set out her family's famous venison pate and placed a few elk tenderloins on the grill knowing they would be ready by the time Libby returned. It was starting to get dark, and Libby should be there any minute. Once the fire was raging, Karl called Peter to inform him of the false alarm. After twenty minutes had passed, Karl began to worry.

"Hey, Sarah, I'm going to walk out and see if I can meet Libby. Maybe she lost track of time."

"Good idea. Take the head lamp and your rifle, just in case."

"All right, I'll be back in a few."

Karl traced Libby's usual route to the creek and called out to her.

"Liberty? Are you there, honey? Libby?"

He waited a few moments and then continued his walk toward the tree grove. With every few steps, he called out her name. When he arrived at the grove, he flashed his light up into the trees but didn't see anything.

"Liberty, honey, are you around here? Please call out if you can hear me."

Karl walked deeper into the grove, where he almost tripped over something. He flashed his light downward and saw what looked like a shoe. He bent down and shone the light closer to the object to determine what it was. He realized, indeed, it was a shoe and, with his gut wrenching, slowly moved the light in the direction of where a face would be. Karl found Liberty.

After falling to his knees, he shook Liberty's shoulders to get her to respond. When that failed, he checked her pulse. He couldn't find one. A father's worst nightmare, his worst nightmare, had come true.

"Oh my God! Oh my God, Liberty, darlin', can you hear me? Talk to me! Say something, please! Please, please, *please!*"

He cried out to God for a miracle or something to make this moment not real.

He sobbed.

Karl, with eyes closed, thought of Sarah.

"Oh my God, Sarah! How am I going to tell her?"

He quickly stood, looked around, attempting to regain his bearings. At that moment, he backed away from Liberty and expelled the contents from his belly, along with his pride. Wiping his eyes, his face, he looked down at his baby girl who was staring up at the darkening sky where stars began to twinkle for the night. He sat next to her, recalling their life together, beginning with the first day he held her as a newborn. It was a homebirthing, and it was the most beautiful event one could ever witness. When she looked him in the eye and clenched his finger, he was hooked and knew he would do anything for her. Tonight, he reached over to close her eyes, pulled his baby into his arms one last time and cried unlike at any other time in his life.

Finally, he mustered the energy to pick her up and carry her home. As he drew closer to the house, he attempted to gather his composure so he could deliver this nightmare to Sarah, somehow. When he made it to the water fountain, he could see Sarah in the house, through the window. Karl stopped to watch her quietly, tears streaming down his face. Sarah radiated peace and he knew this moment would be the last time he would see his beautiful wife in this light. He called out to her, but his voice was only a hoarse whisper.

"Sarah. Sarah!"

This time his call was louder and she heard it. Karl's voice was different. Sarah turned off the stove and ran out onto the porch. Karl was still walking up to the house, and all she could see was his face. It frightened her.

"Hey, babe, are you all right? Where's Liberty? Did you find her?"

"Sarah, I —"

He began to sob. At that point, he was on the other side of the fountain and closer to the porch. Sarah could see he was carrying Libby.

"Oh, Karl, no. Please, no. Libby, is she hurt?"

"She's not breathing, Sare."

Sarah ran out to see for herself, and Karl stopped to lay Liberty gently on the ground next to the fountain because he knew how Sarah would react. When she saw Libby's limp figure, she knew the spirit of Liberty Rose was no longer occupying her body. She stood, frozen. Karl readied himself in case Sarah fainted, which she did. When she came to, she and Karl were sitting on the ground next to Libby. Karl was holding Sarah and crying. Sarah looked back at Liberty and let out a wail. It was haunting, and the shrill sound filled the air. All else grew silent as if all that was natural had stopped to witness and become a part of this tragedy. Sarah cried, holding firmly on to Karl, looking at Liberty in complete disbelief.

"Karl, what happened?"

"I don't know, Sarah. I don't know."

Together they pulled Libby to them, held her in their arms and cried together. As Karl had done earlier, Sarah got up to expel the contents of her belly. Karl reached over to hold her silky hair back and, when she had finished, helped her up. She fell into Karl's arms, dug her face into his chest, and screamed, and sobbed, and screamed again. Together, they held each other and cried until they grew numb.

After a while, Karl walked Sarah into the house and helped her get situated on the chaise. He got a throw blanket to cover her, then went to the phone to dial 9-1-1. He sat on the chaise next to where Sarah was lying. She positioned her head on his lap, and he placed his hand on her head attempting to soothe her pain by gently brushing his fingers through her hair with one hand, holding the phone receiver in the other.

"9-1-1. What's your emergency?"

"Yeah, this is Karl Anderson. I just found my daughter, and she is not breathing. There is no resuscitating her. I don't really know what to do here, but I need to report her death, somehow, and will need a coroner."

"Tell me what happened, Mr. Anderson."

Karl described finding Liberty, sans pulse, as he shared the pertinent details with the operator. He provided his address and phone number. Karl left Sarah lying on the chaise next to the fireplace. She closed her eyes, and from then, the only words she heard were so distant and slow they sounded like myrrh, myrrh, myrrh.

After making the phone call, Karl took another blanket to wrap around Libby's body, then carried her onto the patio, laid her on the chaise and went to pour himself a stiff drink. When the police arrived, he went outside to meet the officers and to recount the gory details of his daughter's passing as best he knew how. Everything felt like slow motion to Karl as he moved through the gestures, repeating the same story, not hearing what was being said. Peter Upchurch arrived at the house and became Karl's eyes and ears. Together, they walked to the tree where Karl had found Liberty lying.

The coroner examined the body and made some sort of statement corroborating Karl's account but said further autopsy would tell the full story. Karl only half heard what was said and just nodded.

The coroner took the body to the morgue for autopsy and stated the body could be released within a day or two for services. Peter noted the details, took all business cards and, after everyone had left for the night, accompanied Karl back into the house.

"This is not what I was expecting to discover when I heard the sirens come onto the property. Is there anything I can do, Karl?"

"Nah, Pete, thank you. Thanks, really."

Before Peter left the house, he covered the platter of tenderloin and other prepared foods and placed everything in the refrigerator. He looked back at Karl and Sarah. Sarah lay on the chaise, and Karl sat on the floor, his head on the cushion of the chaise, Sarah's hand resting on it. Neither was crying; both stared out trying to make sense of what had just happened.

Peter's eyes welled up, and after he closed the front door, he began to cry. Libby had become like a niece to him, and for his wife, Mazy, she was like a little sister. He knew it was going to be an emotional message he would be giving Mazy.

THE NEXT MORNING, the Upchurchs came over to provide support. All appearances indicated Karl and Sarah had slept right where
Peter had left them. Both were wearing the same clothes from the
night before. Karl sat on one side of the chaise, leaning into the
back, eyes closed, while Sarah's head rested on Karl's lap. Sarah
was lying on her side, staring at the fire that had burned cold, like
a once glimmering star that had faded into blackness. They looked
dazed, lost. Mazy called out in a gentle tone, not wanting to wake
Karl, mostly not wanting to startle them, either.

"Morning, may we come in?"

Karl opened his eyes and turned toward Mazy's voice. Peter and
Mazy were standing there with curious compassion. Karl tapped
Sarah's hip as if to say, "Let's get up." Sarah closed her eyes for a
second as if to absorb everything about this moment before she
had to force herself to face this new reality. She sat up slowly and
Karl stood.

"Yes, please, come in. Indeed, it is morning. I suppose we should
get up, maybe make some coffee. Sarah, would you like some coffee?"

"Um, sure, maybe tea instead?"

"Hey, you two sit. I'll make it." Mazy went into the kitchen and
made a light breakfast of toast; coffee; chamomile, lavender and
orange tea; and fresh-squeezed orange juice. Sarah nibbled on the
toast, mostly breathing in the fragrance from the tea, a new mix

she had recently put together. She had dried chamomile flowers and leaves, as well as freshly blooming lavender. Her most recent batch included dried orange peels.

"So, Karl, the police investigator wants to come by today and check things out in the light. If you'd like, I can take care of that for you," Peter said.

"Thanks, Pete, that's a generous offer, but I'd like to check it out myself in the daylight, as well. What time is he supposed to come by?"

"Didn't say. We are supposed to call when we are ready."

"Hmm, okay. Suppose there's no time like the present. Give me a few minutes to wash up, yeah?"

"Sure, I'll call and square away the details."

"All right, thanks! I'll be down in a few minutes."

Peter dialed the number on the detective's card while Karl went upstairs to brush his teeth, take a quick shower and put on fresh clothes as he attempted to garner the strength he needed to face this music. He then forced himself to go down to meet Peter.

"All right Pete, I think I'm ready. Maybe one more cup of coffee. What did the detective say?"

"They'll be here in about half an hour or so."

"All right, cool."

Karl poured another cup of coffee and then went to Sarah and hugged her with his free arm. Sarah leaned in to him, her face resting on his chest, and stood like this while Karl finished his coffee. Mazy and Peter cleaned up the kitchen. Finally, Karl kissed Sarah on the top of her head. Sarah let go of Karl and wiped her eyes.

"All right, Sare, I'll be back."

While Karl and Peter walked to the Thinking Log, Mazy helped Sarah upstairs and into a bath. Mazy could see that Sarah's mind was somewhere else and made a point to keep a close eye as she took incredible care of her. She remained nearby so Sarah would not hurt herself if she fell. She washed Sarah's hair and massaged her head in an attempt to calm her. After the bath, Sarah rubbed moisturizing cream on her face and lotion into her skin, then crawled under the duvet between the softness of fresh linen sheets and pulled the covers over her head. Mazy told Sarah she would be back and ran downstairs, placed some warm buttered toast onto a plate, and poured OJ and a cup of strong valerian root tea. All of this she neatly arranged on one of Sarah's trays. Mazy carried the tray up to Sarah's room.

"Hey, Sarah, this is going to be a crazy week. You're going to need your strength. I brought you some edibles. I also have a cup of valerian root tea if you prefer that instead."

Sarah pulled back the covers and stared at Mazy with a vacant look.

"Did you bring honey for the tea?"

"Yup."

Sarah sat up, ran her fingers through her still-wet hair, and then loosely braided it to one side. Once Sarah thanked Mazy for her graciousness, she crawled back under the covers. Mazy sat on the chaise, trying to read a book as Sarah attempted to fall asleep. Mazy cried, albeit silently.

"Thank you, Mazy."

29

PETER AND KARL SURVEYED THE TREE, trying to understand what had gone wrong. Somewhere in that time, the police investigators came by in attempt to get more details. All agreed the event did not appear to be foul play, but there was a question of whether to label it suicide or accidental.

"Suicide? My daughter was not suicidal. Her life was on track. She finished a dual master's program and was promoted at her job recently. She and her boyfriend are engaged, and we are all planning a big wedding. She's healthy. There is no reason to suspect suicide. What the fuck?!?"

Tensions filled the air. Karl was clearly upset, and Peter was trying to calm him down. Karl turned and walked further away from the house, and especially away from the tree grove, while Peter stayed behind with the officers and answered their remaining questions as best he could. Once the questions were finished, Peter accompanied the officers back to the house and then to their car. The officers thanked Peter and drove away.

Karl moved toward a place of solitude within this expanse of land that was his refuge, where he allowed himself to come to terms with this nightmare. Once he was far enough away from the others, he closed his eyes, tightened his closed fists and let out a scream that echoed across the valley. The depth of his roar caused everything that stirred to pause and witness this deep anguish.

The birds fell silent. Nothing seemed to move: the leaves of the tree stopped swaying; the wind, even the trickle of the creek seemed to stop moving. Karl took several deep breaths before opening his eyes. After quieting himself, he went to the creek to splash his face with water and attempted to regain his composure.

This part of the creek carved into a valley where a wide open pasture was permitted. He sat next to the creek where the sun beamed overhead. His legs were bent for stability, and his arms rested on his knees, hands clenched tightly into fists.

The bubbling of the creek beside him brought up memories. He remembered when he and Sarah made the decision to leave San Francisco in the early 1970s, it was with one requirement, to be near flowing water.

Karl had grown up around the movement of water. It's ebb and flow had become a part of who he was. His childhood home was a forty minute drive from the beach. Together, he and his mother would spend afternoons there, once school ended for the day and while Karl's father was at the office, to watch the surfers. Sometimes they would surf together in areas with smaller waves to catch. Other days it would be simple relaxation and reading at Half Moon Bay. His mother loved the ocean, the sound, the smell, the peace it brought as she breathed in the salt air, and made a point to visit it daily. She lived a life of freedom that came from being outdoors, exploration, and having an open mind. She was happy, had a most peaceful laugh and welcoming smile. This freedom, as well as the peace that came from the movement of water, was what he wanted to provide for his family.

Karl's father was a staunch intellectual and brilliant businessman, one of energy and enthusiasm. He engaged in stimulating conversations that made others question their values, evaluate whether their beliefs were indeed firm and why. He contended there were rules to be followed, especially where societal norms were concerned. He loved to read everything he could get his hands on, encouraging Karl to do the same.

He observed as the world changed, both during and after World War II, when people were becoming more wealthy, including himself. New wars were being started, one in particular whose validity he questioned. He made sure Karl enrolled in a university after high school graduation so he would not be drafted to fight. He watched as his son absorbed the latest hippie lifestyles in his teenage and early adult years, while paying attention to the movement itself, as it grew into a state of revolution against the culture of yesterday, the culture of his father, and his own culture.

While he encouraged his wife's idealism, he made attempts to shape Karl into the kind of man who would see that being in control of your homestead meant having a plan, doing the right thing and honoring God. He guided Karl to look for a good woman, like his mother, and when he found her, to court her with grace, respect and kindness. If she returned the courtesy, then Karl should marry her, have children and create a life that made sense for the family.

He tried to teach Karl that any pursuit of liberty, happiness and prosperity would not be fulfilled by the government alone, or from people fighting against power, but from people taking real action, by taking control and living lives by rules based on the teachings of God.

"Karl, be smart about how you pursue liberty, and know in your heart that being a hippie is more than just a movement. It's a new way of life, a lifestyle that, if taken on, should be done with the courage to follow through. It's evident there is a cultural revolution taking place. It's no longer the values of my father guiding our future, nor are they the values of your father. If you pursue this movement, do it with conviction! Make sure you have a solid life plan. You cannot be lackadaisical.

"Learn how to make money, manage it wisely, and most of all, learn how to live without it, so if the economy falters, you can survive it on your terms. Mismanagement of your funds will place you in a compromising position and possibly make you a permanent slave to the government or corporations so you will never break free. Do not make decisions based on emotion or where money is the only thing holding them together. If you feel a business deal is predicated by an unfair compromise involving money, feel free to walk away. Money should never be the basis for who you are. Nothing worth having will direct you to compromise your integrity, or your self-worth. Love, that is the foundation on which you should establish yourself. You can always make money, but you cannot make someone love you. Know who you are! Know what you stand for, *and dammit, know why*! Know your value!

"Rebellion, revolution, all of that is fine, because nothing stays the same. Hell, man, we just survived the Great Depression, a Dust Bowl and Second World War and the aftereffect is change. Women who started to make a real living wage during the war don't want to give that up, nor should they. Black people, and other minorities, are fighting for civil liberties justly deserved. It's time for this revolution for the love of our community and society as a whole. It's the right time!

"Keep your claws sharp. Never stop learning and paying attention to what is going on around you, because when that wind of change shifts, you do not want to be caught off guard. Just be smart! Do not burn the house down.

"Most importantly, find your grounding, Son, so you are not forced to compromise who you are, at the core; otherwise you are a lost kite blowing in the wind. If you are not sure how to do this, then lean on me. I will help guide you. If I am not here, then do what I do: lean on my God for direction."

Karl could feel the harsh winds of change now and was searching for reason to understand Libby's demise. It was these words of wisdom spoken by his father, during a Saturday hike to Rodeo Beach, beneath the Golden Gate Bridge, that resonated in his mind. That conversation was one of the most cherished memories of his adult life. It was this conversation that had really pushed Karl to consider the full meaning behind liberty, and the pursuit of this state of being a free man. It was this conversation Karl had referenced when deciding to leave San Francisco, to create a life for his family, which led him and Sarah here, near Telluride. He remembered the day when Sarah said she was pregnant, the happiness he felt the day Liberty was born and when his daughter first noticed him. He had been happy when Sarah agreed to name her Liberty. Her name was a reminder of this conversation with his father.

In truth, he missed his dad, as well as his mom, greatly, and yearned for their words of wisdom in this, his worst life experience. Both of his parents had died in a tragic car accident during a weekend getaway near Mendocino a couple of years after that day. It was the same year Karl was sure he wanted to marry Sarah. She had the privilege of meeting his parents once.

As sole heir, Karl was left with all of his father's savings. The amount was in the low millions. Karl left the money alone, completely untouched, until he could understand how to manage that kind of asset. The responsibility that came with that amount was daunting. Ultimately, Karl returned to school and received his master's degree in business finance. The first time he spent any funds from the Anderson Family Trust was for the family refuge in southern Colorado.

Immediately, images flashed of the day he and Sarah selected this lot. He remembered how vacant it was where there is now a home, a garden and a barn full of animals. Images of Liberty growing up by the creek, in the grove, with the animals, flooded his mind. Karl was grateful for having had the opportunity to provide this environment for his family.

In some way, sitting here near the creek, lamenting the death of Liberty, he felt the presence of his parents closer to him, as if his father were standing behind him giving him the strength and courage he needed to hold on, and the peace of his mother sitting next to him, embracing the ebb and flow of the creek and the sun as it comforted his soul. When he felt his strength return, Karl stood and followed the path home to be with Sarah.

AS NIGHT FELL ON THE FIRST DAY, Karl and Sarah lay in bed. This moment was the first opportunity for Karl to absorb all he had taken in. He closed his eyes, and the room started to spin. Once his equilibrium became more normalized, he moved closer toward Sarah, and they folded into each other. He kissed the back of her head and lay there for a few moments more, in silence, before stating the obvious.

"Sarah, we will need to start planning an end-of-life celebration."

"I know, Karl. I just don't know how I'm going to—how am I going to tell people my only child is gone?"

"Yeah, I don't know how to accept it myself."

"So, what happened with our sweet Liberty, Karl?"

"Well, as best as I can tell, it appears she somehow lost her balance and fell from the Thinking Log. That was where she was lying when I found her last night."

"Did she suffer?"

"I don't think so. The coroner says it appears she died instantly."

"Mmm."

"Sarah, where shall we bury her? Under the old oak? Or in the spot we set aside as the family burial plot?"

Sarah sighed loudly. "Liberty should be buried in the family plot, but we should plant a memorial at the Thinking Log."

"I like that."

With that decided, Sarah and Karl fell asleep.

31

THE NEXT MORNING, Karl and Peter began digging out the burial site. Mazy and Sarah went to select a coffin and a dress for Liberty to be buried in. That was enough for Sarah, who suggested the rest she and Karl would need to do together, like going to the coroner's office, identifying the body and other heart-wrenching tasks. Mazy drove Sarah back home in silence.

Later that morning, Mazy, Sarah and Karl began calling family members and friends to share the terrible news. Karl agreed to call Libby's employer, as well as Adam. Karl focused on the easiest, least emotional conversation, Libby's employer.

"Oh my goodness. This is unexpected news. She asked for some time off saying she had to return to Colorado for a family emergency. Is everything else okay?"

Karl was unsure what to say and suddenly realized there was more to Libby's visit than he knew.

"Well, thank you for asking, Tom. At this time, other than Liberty's unfortunate circumstance, nothing else is relevant. We are planning an end-of-life celebration for Liberty. It will take place three days from now, here in Colorado. If any of you are able to come, you are all welcome."

Karl gave the location and other details and then disconnected. He was puzzled about the reasoning Libby had given for her time off. What was going on? He looked at Sarah to see how she was doing. They smiled weary smiles at each other. Next was Adam. Maybe Adam could help give some answers. Karl took a deep breath. This was going to be the hardest call to make. He had never prepared himself for relaying news to his daughter's fiancé of her death. He took another deep breath. Sarah walked over and kissed him on the top of his head.

"You're going to do fine, Karl."

Karl picked up the phone and dialed Adam's number. It rang three times before going to voice mail.

"Um, hey, Adam, it's Karl Anderson, Liberty's father. There was an accident, uh, with Liberty. Please call us here at the house when you get this message. It's urgent."

Karl gave the telephone number and set the phone down.

After lunch, Karl and Sarah drove down to the coroner's office.

"Well, Mr. and Mrs. Anderson, we have finished the autopsy. It was difficult to determine whether she fell on purpose or in an accident."

"On purpose, what? Karl, I don't understand."

"Look, Doc, as I explained to the officer, Liberty—"

"Yes, I know. I don't mean to interrupt, but I read the report where you explained all of the positive things taking place in her life. That is why I have decided to label the death accidental."

"Thank you, Doc. We appreciate that."

"I also wanted to let you know, as custom, we take tox screens to determine whether drugs may have played a part. We discovered marijuana in her blood. That may have been a contributor, but it's hard to say." He paused before adding, "Miss Anderson was also pregnant. I thought you should know."

"What? Pregnant?" Karl and Sarah asked at the same time and looked at each other with even deeper heartbreak. Sarah reached over for Karl and pulled herself closer as if to hold on firmly to an anchor.

"Yes. She may not have known about it. At least I am hoping she did not know, considering she had been using."

"Right, thank you for telling us. So, what do we need to do next?" Karl asked.

"Talk to Lupita at the front desk. Please let her know what we should do for funeral arrangements."

Their next stop was at the funeral home. Although Liberty would be buried at home, they wanted a professional embalming. Mostly, they wanted Liberty to look better than she had on the slab in the coroner's office. The funeral director agreed to make arrangements to pick up the body from the coroner's office, do the embalmment work and drive Liberty home closer to the date. The Andersons paid the fee and drove home.

"Karl, did you get in touch with Adam?"

"No. He didn't pick up. I left him a voice mail."

"I'll call his mother. Do you think he knew about the pregnancy, Karl?"

"I'm not sure, darlin'."

Karl wondered what had happened between Adam and Liberty. Why did Liberty feel the need to lie to her employer about coming home? What was the family emergency? Was it the pregnancy? Had she come home to give them the news in person? Where in the hell was Adam? Why wasn't he calling back?

"Thanks, Sarah, that's a great idea. When you talk to Diane, ask her where in the fuck her son is."

Karl couldn't wait to talk to Adam. He was growing angry and wanted answers. He reached out and held Sarah's hand as if to apologize for being so curt. She looked at him. Everyone was hurting.

After the pregnancy news, the hurt went just a little deeper than it had the day before. She kissed his hand. Karl turned up the volume of the last CD and song he had been listening to, Portishead, "Western Eyes." The CD had been a gift from Liberty. Other than Pink Floyd, this was her favorite band.

"You'll love it, Dad!" Liberty had said. "This album is quickly becoming a favorite. Of course, the first album is the absolute best, but this one is pretty great, too!"

The rest of the drive home was spent in somber tranquility as tunes from the Portishead disc filled the air.

32

ADAM WAS STANDING ON A PATIO overlooking the Pacific Ocean, contemplating whether or not to go out and surf. He was venturing closer to not as he stood watching the timing of the wave sets, while seeking solace with The Reverend, a Belgian-inspired brew from Avery, a Colorado-based brewery. It was a favorite beer, especially now, as he was reeling inside with what he and Liberty were dealing with. He needed comforting, and since he didn't have a church of his own, silent confessions made before each sip of The Rev, in hopes of making amends, were good enough for him. Although it was early in the day, seeing Karl's missed call had made him want to drink a beer instead of coffee. Finally, he checked his voice mail and listened to Karl's message.

"Um, hey, Adam, it's Karl Anderson, Liberty's father. There was an accident, uh, with Liberty. Please call us here at the house when you get this message. It's urgent—."

He wasn't ready to return the call. He wasn't ready to talk to Karl, or to anyone for that matter, about his relationship status with Liberty. Even so, he was concerned about what might have happened to Liberty and knew he would have to return the call as soon as possible. At that moment, two hands slid around his hard stomach.

"Hey, Adam, are you going out?"

Adam looked down at her, at Mandi, the girl he had thought was "the one" while at UNC. She looked up at him, teasing him by lightly rubbing her finger on his chest and pulling herself in closer to him. Adam smiled at her and took another drink of his beer. He looked back out to the ocean, to his cell phone, then to Mandi.

"No, I don't think so. Maybe later."

"Good. Come back to bed. I want to show you a new move."

This piqued Adam's interest and he obeyed. Mandi pulled on the drawstring of his cotton pants, led him from the patio back into the house and started her foreplay immediately. Adam placed his cell on the nearest table, telling himself he would return that call — after.

33

LIBBY'S TEST RESULTS CAME BACK to Dr. Whiteman's office with all of the other lab results. The clerk separated Libby's from the others, made a copy to mail to Liberty's home address, as was custom, and proceeded to hole punch the top of the original so it could be placed in her patient folder. She stapled the copy and used the yellow highlighter to highlight the results, on both the copy and the original. Once her work was complete, she picked up the envelopes with lab result letters and placed them in the mail stop bin so the cute postman, who stopped by at 4:30 every afternoon, could pick them up. She had a small crush on him. It was no secret to anyone in the office as she always found a moment to take a break from whatever she was doing to be around when he came by.

She vowed to herself she would return at 4:30 that afternoon to see him. She then picked up the patient folders and placed them on Dr. Whiteman's desk in two piles. One pile was for positive, or abnormal, results, and the second pile was for negative, or normal, results.

Between patient consults, Dr. Whiteman read the lab results and made her own piles. Her first one was "needs additional research" and "possible prescription or follow-up appointment"; the second pile indicated quick phone calls to provide results. While she was sorting the patient records, she picked up the folder for Liberty Rose Anderson. She remembered Liberty's fiancé had reportedly been diagnosed with AIDS and that she was frazzled about the possibility she, too, might have AIDS. Dr. Whiteman quickly scanned to the highlighted result and saw the typed word "negative." She then read the rest of Libby's results and noticed all of her blood work was normal; T-cells, WBC and RBC were perfectly in the normal range.

"Hallelujah. This is great news."

The doctor had a habit of talking to herself when reviewing the charts. She looked at the extra blood work she had ordered, HGH, and saw it was positive. Libby was positively pregnant. She looked up Libby's phone number and called her. There was no answer, so as directed, she left a voice-mail message.

"Hello, Miss Anderson, it's Hannah Whiteman. We have your blood work results in, and I have some good news for you. For starters, you do not have HIV or AIDS, so you can rest easy, about that, anyway. I have some other news for you. It appears you *are* pregnant. When you return home, let's get together and talk about the next nine months. Have a great day!"

Of course, Liberty would never receive this news. She would never know the truth.

34

WHEN KARL AND SARAH returned home, they noticed the rental car Libby had left. The instant anticipation, and immediate heartbreak, the car symbolized ignited deeper anguish. They had forgotten all about it, and when they saw it again, tears welled up in their eyes.

"Karl, get rid of that car," Sarah said. "I don't want to see it anymore."

Karl didn't respond, but he agreed; the car was an eyesore. Sarah entered the house, and Karl went to the car and opened the door in hope of finding the keys, or any paper work, so he could determine the rental company. The keys were still in the ignition and Karl removed them. On the key fob, he saw the words "TelluAir Car Rental" and a phone number. Before getting out, he looked around to make sure there was nothing belonging to Libby. On the passenger floorboard, he noticed a business card. It was for a Dr. Hannah Whiteman, Internal Medicine. The back of the card read, "Call for test results in two days."

"Thank you, Liberty, I will."

Karl stepped out of the car with the key fob and business card and went into the house.

"Did Adam return my call?"

"No. I talked with his mother. They are driving down and will be here tonight. I told them they could stay here."

"Good. Has she heard from Adam?"

"No, not yet."

"Well, I found a number to call for the car. I also found this business card."

Karl handed the card to Sarah. She read the front: "Dr. Hannah Whiteman, Internal Medicine, La Jolla, California."

"Turn it over. Read the back."

Sarah turned the card over.

"'Call for test results in two days.' What could this be for? Oh, Karl, Libby must have thought she was pregnant and took a test. I wonder why she went to an internal medicine doctor and not her women's health practitioner."

"I'm not sure, but we need to call the doctor to see what results Libby was expecting. She apparently informed her office she was coming home to deal with a family emergency. Do you know anything about that?"

"A family emergency? Hmm, no, I don't know anything about that."

"All right, well, announcing a pregnancy on the spur of the moment isn't like Libby. She would have planned a trip out here with Adam, and everyone would have known they were coming. It would have been an event. If we don't hear back from Adam soon, we need to call this doctor. Maybe she can help us understand why Liberty came home."

"Let's wait until after. Okay, Karl? Dealing with her death is proving to be difficult. Now I have to wrap my head around the fact we have lost our only daughter and our only opportunity of having a grandchild. Let me come to terms with this first."

Karl looked at Sarah and sighed deeply. She was right. This was a lot to deal with. Karl picked up the phone and called the number on the back of the key fob.

"TelluAir Car Rental, how may I help you?"

"Hello, my daughter, Liberty Anderson, rented a car from you recently. We need to know where to return it."

"Let me look that up. Do you have the rental agreement number?"

"No. I only have my daughter's name, Liberty Anderson."

"Ah, yes, found it. She rented the 2006 Toyota Camry two days ago from the Telluride Airport. She can return it here."

"Uh-huh, we would like to return it as soon as possible. Where exactly shall we drop it off?"

"If it is easiest for you, we can pick it up at your location if you'd like."

"Really? Yes, thank you, that would be great."

Karl gave his address with directions and phone number so someone from TelluAir Car Rental could pick up the car. He set down the phone and looked at Sarah.

"They'll be here later this afternoon to pick up the rental car."

"Great. Thank you, honey."

35

MAZY AND PETER TOOK CARE of all of the details for Liberty's end-of-life celebration. Peter finished digging the grave, and Mazy picked fresh herbs and flowers for beautiful arrangements. Together, she and Pete tried to make it easy for Karl and Sarah to come to terms with this horrific event. She loved Liberty as if she were her own little sister, and she was heartbroken.

Karl and Sarah were the parents Mazy claimed. Sarah had been the mother figure Mazy wished her own mother had been, and she would do anything for the Andersons. Sarah had taught Mazy how to plant and keep a garden, how to can food and how to cook. Mazy confided all of her secrets to Sarah, her biggest being that Mazy was not sure she wanted to have children of her own and wondered if she was being selfish about holding back. Sarah comforted Mazy, assuring her that, as a woman, she had a choice to carry a child, or not. And if she was not sure, then the best decision would be to not, considering the responsibility that comes with being a mom is more than simply birthing a child. She also encouraged Mazy to be honest with Peter about what she was feeling. Which she did during one of their day hikes. They had reached their summit and were eating peanut butter and jelly sandwiches. Peter was awesome about it.

"Hey, Petey, so I was thinking about having kids."

"Yeah? And, are you wanting to try?"

Peter started to snuggle with Mazy, and after she returned his kiss, she smiled.

"Well, I'm not sure. I am thinking I may not want children."

"Now or ever?"

"Well, maybe not ever. Is that bad? I feel like I may be selfish in not wanting them, like I may be holding you back from something you want."

"Darlin', I married you because I love you for everything you are, and for everything you are not. I respect you, Mazy. You are my wife, my life partner. If we decide whether or not to have children, know that we are in this together, you and me, whatever it turns out to be. Thank you for telling me. I would have gone crazy trying to figure this out."

"I love you, Peter. Thank you."

Mazy and Peter had been nineteen years old when they left Missouri. They had eloped after high school graduation at the mature age of eighteen. Mazy's parents had been beside themselves with anxious confusion. It was confusing to see their firstborn child marry the first man she met. Mazy's parents hated Peter immediately. Actually, it was Mazy's mother who had hated Peter, and she attempted to break apart the relationship by insisting he would never amount to anything, since he was uneducated. After a year of unsuccessful attempts, Mazy's mother demanded Mazy and Peter annul the marriage or Mazy would be out of the family. Of course, this had the opposite effect, because Mazy chose Peter.

Peter and Mazy had enough savings to drive to Northern California and create a new life there. It wouldn't be a grand life, not immediately, but it would be their life. It would be a happy life, on their terms. They recognized it would be a rough road, but if they remained committed to their love, they could make it with a family of their own.

During their drive west, they entered Colorado and decided to go off the beaten path to see more of a state they were starting to fall in love with. That was when they drove through Telluride, near where Karl and Sarah lived. It was starting to get dark, and they realized they would need to find a place to camp soon.

"Check it, Peter. Their gate is open, and the light is on. Maybe it's a sign this should be our new home."

Peter chuckled and continued to drive.

"It's beautiful here, Mazy, but we can't afford to live here. Did you see that small town we passed through? Where would we work? Keep looking for signs of a campsite."

"We could work for those people whose gate is open. Come on, Petey, let's check it out. I have a great feeling about this place. It feels like home. If they say no, we can go with our original plan, find a camp spot and continue our drive to Northern California in the morning."

"Aargh, fine, Mazy. This is nuts, but let's check it out."

"Yay, thanks, Petey. We are going to be so happy here. I just know it."

"Maybe, darlin'."

Peter pulled through the Anderson family gate and coasted slowly up the long, dark drive toward their home. As they drew closer to the house, they could see a faint path leading away from the house into the forest. The pathway sparkled, as though a shimmer of fairy dust had been sprinkled around. It was another sign to Mazy they were home. She smiled and felt giddy with excitement. Peter laughed and embraced her positive energy as his own. He started to agree with Mazy; this indeed could be home.

The water fountain was lit up, an indicator they were close to the house. There were two distinctly lit pathways. One led to the back of the house, the other to a circular drive in the front. Peter turned off the ignition, and through the window, he and Mazy could see the Anderson family laughing and eating dinner.

"See, Petey, this is a happy place."

Peter sighed and looked at Mazy. He chuckled again and reached over to kiss her.

"You know this is stupid crazy, don't you, Mazy? If he comes out with a shotgun . . ."

"Honey, look at them. They look like happy hippies. They aren't going to shoot us. They probably don't even own a gun."

With that, Peter got out of the car, went up to the porch and knocked on the front door. Mazy climbed out of the car also and stood by the porch so she could be seen as a friendly, nonthreatening wife. When they heard the knocking, Karl looked at Sarah, and Sarah looked at Karl.

"Are you expecting anyone, Sare?"

"Uh, no. Libby, sweetie, are you expecting anyone?"

"Yes."

"You are? Who are you expecting, darlin'?"

"The tooth fairy. I lost a tooth. Wanna see?"

They all laughed.

"Well, let me go greet the tooth fairy. You two stay here, okay?"

"All right, Daddy."

Karl quietly got up to grab the shotgun from the closet and went to the front door. Before he got there, he saw a small, fully packed Volkswagen Westfalia through the window. It was white and had Missouri plates. A young woman was standing at the bottom of the porch stairs, and a young man was standing at the door. They looked like kids. Karl kept the shotgun hidden in his left hand and opened the front door with his right.

"Hello, are you lost?"

"Uh, hello, sir, my name is Peter Upchurch. My wife, Mazy, and I were driving through the area on our way to California. We were looking for a place to camp, and we noticed your gate was open."

Peter turned to point to his wife, expecting her to be in the van, and saw she was standing at the bottom stair. He looked at her with widened eyes as if to say, "What are you doing?" and Mazy raised her hand to wave. It was a giddy, excitable wave.

"Hi, I'm Mazy, Peter's wife. You have a lovely home."

Karl smiled, set down the shotgun and went out onto the porch. Peter stepped back.

"Where are you kids from?"

"Mazy and I are from St. Louis, Missouri. We've been married for a year, and we decided we wanted to start the rest of our life together in Northern California."

Mazy climbed up the stairs to join her husband. She hooked her arm in his and listened cheerfully, nodding in agreement.

"The problem is, we fell in love with Colorado, this part of Colorado specifically, and we've decided to live here."

"Uh-huh, so what do your parents say about this?"

"Sir, I don't mean any sort of disrespect, but as this fine woman's husband, it is my responsibility to take care of my wife. It is my personal ambition to do that to the best of my ability."

"All right, I can respect that. So, you're looking for a spot to camp?"

"Yes, and a job. Would you be interested in letting us live here on your land? Mazy and I will help maintain whatever needs maintaining, the animals, your house, your farm, in return for a place to live and food for our family, possibly an income."

"How many of you make up your family?"

"Just the two of us right now. We won't get in your way."

"Tell you what, Peter, why don't you two set up your tent and camp here for the night? There is a creek about a hundred feet from here; just follow that path. We can revisit this with my wife in the morning. She makes a scrumptious breakfast, so be here somewhat early."

"Thank you, uh. . ."

"Karl. My name is Karl. Do you have a flashlight?"

"Yes. We do. Thank you, Karl."

"So much. Thank you, so much," Mazy added.

Peter and Karl shook hands, and the young couple turned to unpack their camping gear from the Westfalia. Mazy jumped on Peter's back and squeezed him tightly. Karl snickered, recognizing their young love as the real deal, and went back into the house.

That had been twenty-five years ago.

Once the family plot was prepared, Mazy took a picture with her new digital camera. She went into the main house to check on Sarah.

"Sarah?"

"In here, sweetie."

"Here's a picture of the plot. Are you all right with it?"

Sarah was in the main living room, sitting in front of a burning fire, with a blanket draped over her legs. She was holding a cup of her blend of chamomile, lavender and orange tea. Sarah looked at the picture and smiled sadly.

"Absolutely. It's beautiful. Thank you so much, Mazy. I don't know how we would have managed this without you and Peter. I am so glad you are here."

36

ADAM LAY IN BED THINKING about Libby and the return call he needed to make to Karl. He turned and saw Mandi's perfectly shaped body as she lay there, naked, sleeping. Mandi had located Adam in early November. She had received his number from someone they had both known in college and had called him. The call was a complete surprise to Adam, and they agreed to meet for lunch in Del Mar. Libby was traveling quite a bit with her new job, and Adam didn't think she would mind, especially considering they would be getting married soon. Adam loved Libby anyway and wouldn't do anything to hurt her. Then he saw Mandi. She was even more beautiful than he remembered, and previous emotions reemerged. Mandi's beauty was far different from Libby's all-natural beauty. Mandi showed off her screamingly perfect figure with formfitting clothes, wore makeup, and her hair was always styled. She looked, smelled and felt like fresh air. With that first lunch, Adam remembered why he had thought Mandi was the one. It was because she was. Mandi was the one who made him want to be a better man.

Liberty was awesome, and he loved her, but she was more like the best friend, the young veggie sister, who would accept Adam regardless of what he did or who he was, even if he failed. Adam felt Libby had an idealistic view of what a relationship was. He blamed that on her parents, who were idealists themselves. Adam felt Karl and Sarah had done Liberty a disservice by homeschooling her and by being perfectly in love all the time. That wasn't what things were like in the real world. People were not really as happy and in love as Karl and Sarah pretended to be. Of course, Adam never let Libby know he thought that. Over the years, he had been looking for ways to let Liberty down gently, but he knew she was completely in love with him. Each time he let go of her, he went to look for Mandi, or someone like her.

When he became discouraged, he would go back to Libby to see how she was doing. She was always so excited to see him, and with no real effort, they would be back together again. The last time he came back, he decided it was time to settle down, even if that meant settling with Liberty. She loved him and, actually, he loved her enough.

Lunches with Mandi started happening frequently, followed by dinners, nights at her place and very little sleeping. After about a month of their excursions, he told Mandi he and Libby, his girlfriend from UNC, were living together.

"What? I thought that was over."

"It was. It started back up again."

"End it, Adam, or we're done."

"It's not going to be that easy, Mandi. For one, she's always traveling. For another, we are supposed to go away for Christmas with our parents. It's been planned for months. I'll tell her when we return."

Of course, he didn't tell Mandi about the engagement. Truly, that was what made leaving Libby so difficult. How would he break the news to Libby? To his parents? This was truly fucked up.

"Fine, for now, Adam; just come over here and make me scream."

Adam sighed now and decided he needed to call Karl. If Liberty was in the hospital, he would need to make an appearance. He pulled on a pair of shorts, opened another bottle of The Rev to lean on for sacred strength and comfort. He picked up his phone and returned to the patio. After drinking half the beer, he placed the bottle on the ledge. He dialed the number Karl had left on his voice mail, leaned on the ledge and took in the view.

After two rings, Karl answered.

"Karl Anderson."

"Karl, it's me. I called as soon as I got your message. Is Liberty okay? You have me worried."

"Adam, so glad you called. Where in the fuck are you? You need to get your ass to Colorado." Karl paused for a minute, realizing how pissed off he was at Adam. He paused to take a deep breath, mellowed his tone and said, "There is no easy way to tell you this, Adam, so here it goes. Liberty died two nights ago. I have questions and I am certain you have answers. We will bury her in two days. You should be here."

"Wait, what? Liberty—what? Was it suicide?"

"Why in the fuck would she commit suicide, Adam?"

"I—I don't know. I don't know why I said that. Yeah, of course, I'll be there. I'll fly in tomorrow. Karl, how did it happen? What happened?"

"Be here tonight. We can talk about it then. Your parents are on their way."

"Yeah, sure. See you tonight."

Adam stepped back in disbelief. He covered his mouth and then held his head as though it might explode. The phone dropped out of his hand and broke apart into fragmented pieces.

"Oh, fuck! Fuck. Fuck. Fuck. Liberty, what in the hell did you do?"

He ran back into the house to shower, dress and pack. He drove to the San Diego airport where he paid through the nose for the next available flight to Colorado. Before leaving, he'd scrawled a few words together to make a note to Mandi.

It read, "Family emergency—CO. Be back soon. A"

37

THAT EVENING, HOURS AFTER HIS conversation with Adam, Karl poured himself a glass of rum with a splash of cola. It had been a perplexing couple of days. First Liberty's death, then her employer asking about a family emergency that didn't exist, the coroner saying Libby was pregnant, the business card Karl held in his hand about test results and now Adam mentioning suicide. What had been going on with Liberty? What was the family emergency? All of these questions were making Karl feel dizzy with confusion. He was taking a sip of his heavy concoction, thinking it would stabilize his unsteady thoughts, when he remembered Libby's cell phone. He pulled it out of his pocket, flipped it open and noticed she had a missed call. A little envelope image also appeared, indicating a new voice mail. He saw that the phone number on the cell phone display matched the phone number on the business card. He pushed the button programmed to dial voice mail, and a recording with Libby's voice came up.

"Libby Anderson."

The voice mail announcement was like an announcement to the self confirming you are who you think you are or, in Karl's case, who his daughter was. It was followed by four words Karl did not want to hear.

"Please enter your password."

"Shit."

Karl did not know Libby's password, and just as he started to make attempts, Sarah called out to him.

"Karl, we have visitors. I think it's Diane, Adam's mother."

Karl powered off the cell phone to save the battery and put it back in his pocket. He swallowed the entirety of his drink and went to the front door to see it was Adam, along with his mother, Diane, and his father, Richard, who had arrived.

"Hey, you are all together?" Karl asked.

"Yeah, Adam called us from the San Diego airport saying he was catching the next flight out. We told him we'd pick him up, and so, here we are."

"Please, come in. Do you have any bags? Do you need help?"

"No, we're good. We brought our bags up," said Richard.

"Great, come in."

Everyone shuffled into the house. Karl and Rich took the bags up to the guest rooms. Karl hesitated and then placed Adam's bags in Libby's room. Adam and Diane went into the combination family room and kitchen, where Mazy and Peter were sitting on the sofa. Sarah went to Adam, hugged him tightly and began to cry. Adam returned the hug, closing his eyes in complete disgrace.

"Sarah, I am so sorry. This was so unexpected. I am so, so sorry. You know how much I love Liberty."

Sarah cried a little more.

"Oh, Adam, I know. Liberty loved you very much, too. Her wedding dress arrived a few days ago. I have it hanging in her room. Neither one of us will get to see her wearing it now."

Diane and Adam looked at each other and she went to Sarah to give her a big hug, relieving Adam. He noticed Peter and Mazy sitting on the sofa and smiled sadly; they all said hello. Adam moved to the patio door and looked out. Tears welled up in his eyes, and he wiped them away. He really wanted a stiff drink. Moments later, Karl approached and placed his hand on Adam's shoulder, squeezing it tightly. Adam turned to look at Karl. There were still tears in Adam's eyes.

"Karl, I am so sorry about Liberty. This is not the news I was expecting to hear today. I am so sorry."

"Thank you, Adam. It wasn't the kind of news I ever expected to be sharing, much less come to terms with. It's been rough."

Karl took a deep breath and refrained from asking Adam any questions. It had been one convoluted couple of days, so instead, he returned to the counter and began to fix everyone a drink. The night's concoction was rum with a splash of cola and a lime garnish. Sarah and the ladies opted for wine instead.

"So, Karl, what happened?" Adam asked.

Adam looked at Karl intently, really wanting to know what had happened to Liberty. Karl looked at Adam, wanting to ask him the same question. Both would be expecting different answers. Karl wanted to know what tests Libby had taken, why and what drove her to come home. Instead, Karl decided he would wait until he got Adam alone.

"Well, she fell thirty feet from the old oak tree in the grove, Adam."

"Oh my God! Did she say anything before? Was she upset?"

"No, she didn't, at least not that we know of. No one was home when Liberty fell. In fact, neither Sarah nor I were expecting her to be here. Do you know why Liberty came home, Adam?"

"No, she didn't say. I've been working a lot on this project. I, uh, I don't know why she came here without telling anyone."

"Weren't you worried? She's been here for a couple of days."

"No, yeah, no. No, I thought she might have been pulled away on a work trip. When I called her, it went straight to voice mail."

Karl recalled all numbers and stored names from the missed call log on Libby's flip phone and recognized Adam was lying. Karl then looked at Sarah. She was swilling the wine in her glass and looking down as the wine swirled just below the rim. It was clear she did not want to talk, at least not at this moment.

"So, we arrived home, noticed a strange car sitting in our driveway, and when we came in, we found a note on the counter saying she had gone for a walk. It was close to sunset when Sarah and I started to prepare dinner. When she didn't come home by sunset, we grew concerned. That is when I went to look for her and when I found her lying beneath the oak."

Adam and Karl just looked at each other. Karl could tell Adam was hiding something, and Adam could feel Karl's stare bore deep into the fragile crevices of his soul. Adam wiped his eyes. He felt guilty. He wanted to know if Libby had left any other kind of note, but didn't want to bring up the idea of suicide again.

"Ah, this is a lot to bear for one day," Adam said. "I'm not feeling well. If you all will excuse me, I'd like to go to bed."

Sarah stood and went to Adam. She gave him another hug, and Adam sobbed in her arms. Peter and Mazy stood and began to excuse themselves. They picked up the empty glasses and carried them to the sink, washed and placed them in the dish rack. Karl and Sarah thanked them and bid them a good night. Sarah then looked at her guests and at Karl.

"Like Adam, I, too, am not feeling well. Tomorrow is going to be a busy day. I think I may go to bed also."

With that, everyone decided going to bed was the best idea, and the second day ended.

38

ADAM CLIMBED THE STAIRS to Libby's room and stood at the doorway, leaning against the doorjamb. The table lamp had been turned on, illuminating the essence that made up Liberty's room. He remembered the first time she had brought him here. As if he were transported back in time, he could see, hear and smell sweet Liberty Rose. On that day, she had led him up the stairs to her room, hooking her fingers into his. The moment had been stressful, and he hadn't been sure how her parents were going to take the news about the pregnancy. Adam had been more nervous than ever. The lightness of Libby made it easier to bear. Although he believed Libby was not ready to be a mother, he admired the way she handled the matter with such grace, which made Adam want to be a part of her life. When they reached her room, she turned to look at him. It was the first time Liberty had ever shown Adam to her room. She smiled and then laughed giddily.

"Well, this is it. Are you ready to step into my little indoor hideaway?"

Libby let go of his finger and did a twist jump onto her bed, landing in a seated position. Everything on her bed bounced as the springs in her mattress caught her. Her hair moved with lightness; her eyes closed softly and then slowly reopened. She laughed like a child, which made Adam smile. She placed both palms facedown on the duvet and moved her hands forward and back as if making butterfly wing shapes in the fabric. She was still smiling, and he could see she was reading his reaction with her inquisitive eyes. She looked around, as if seeing her room for the first time, through his eyes. Slowly, she looked back at Adam.

"Come in, silly. Sit by me."

Adam chuckled and then followed her steps. He jumped on the bed, pulling her back into a lying position. They laughed, and when they stopped, they turned to look at one another. Adam smiled at her, took her hand and kissed it.

"So, this is where you grew up?"

"Yup, a little slice of my history."

Tonight, as Adam leaned against the doorjamb, he looked around, and he could see the spirit of Libby radiating in and around the room, which touched him deep within his soul. There were pictures of her with people she loved, her friends and family. There were other pictures of her young self, cuddling with her rabbits, kissing her dogs, and one poignant picture of little Liberty Rose on her Thinking Log. She was gazing out pensively at the lower Rockies, of course, thinking.

Then he saw the photos of Libby and himself at different stages of their lives together. That was what drew him in, and when he stepped into the room. The photos in separate frames were of the two of them. Each one captured a keen moment, such as when she first moved into his apartment. Others had been taken at favorite campsites and cool summit points. Tears streamed from his eyes. He looked away and there it was, her wedding dress. Seeing it was like a solid punch in the gut. He gasped as if trying to find his breath. The dress was beautiful, and he could suddenly see Libby wearing it. Startled, Adam stepped back and almost tripped.

Like Lady Macbeth, Adam broke down out of guilt.

39

ADAM DID NOT REMEMBER falling asleep, but when he woke up, he was fully clothed, on a fully made bed, with the lamp still on. He considered he might be in a hypnopompic state, where his body was still in sleep mode, but his mind was considering if all of this was real or just a dream. It was a feeling of being cold that had jolted him into this conscious moment. This wasn't like a normal feeling of cold. This was like after experiencing a cold sweat. It was clammy and uncomfortable, and all Adam wanted was to become warm again. He removed his socks and the rest of his clothing, crawled under the blankets, and turned off the lamp.

He pulled the blankets completely over his head so he could stop seeing all things Libby. He yearned for the blackness, and warmth, this soft blanket tent might provide. The tent first gave him the blackness he yearned for, to match what he felt inside his heart, until he closed his eyes. Then, it was as if someone flipped a switch and a Libby documentary began to play as streaming images filled a screen on the backdrop of his mind.

He could hear her laugh. He could hear her voice calling to him, the same voice that always drew him back to her. He could see the beauty of Libby and her bouncing brown hair, her sparkling blue eyes and the smile that made him want to move closer, just to be a part of her. She radiated like the sun. She brought the light into his dark sky. She was so fucking beautiful, natural; Adam decided at that moment that Liberty Rose Anderson was the most beautiful woman he would ever be fortunate to know. Each new memory was like the nipple a mother placed in the mouth of a crying babe. Adam had never cried like this; hell, he couldn't remember ever crying, but he did, cry, on this night. Under the blanket tent, he could see Liberty plain as day. He could hear her; smell, taste and feel her.

"I'm sorry, Liberty."

Adam whispered this apology over and over again, and in his mind, he could hear her softly repeating the "Shhh" sound. He felt her hand on his head, gently smoothing his hair, the way she always did. It was calming. Slowly, the light from his memory faded, and he was able to fall asleep.

"I love you, Liberty. I do."

"Shhhh—"

40

WHEN ADAM AWOKE, he could feel the dry scratch against his eyes. His head hurt and he felt as if he were hungover. Quickly his eyes opened and he looked around. He then saw the wedding dress and remembered he was in Libby's room. He then remembered she was not there with him. Waking up fully, he pulled off the blankets, threw on some fresh clothes and went to the bathroom to splash his face. He leaned on the sink for a minute looking at his reflection in the mirror. His eyes were swollen, red, and there was no sign of a smile. When he tried to fake a smile, he couldn't do it. At that moment, Adam did not recognize himself. He turned away, and instead of returning to Libby's room, he went down the stairs into the kitchen, made a fresh pot of coffee and, when it was ready, poured a cup and walked out to the patio to sit, hoping the coldness of the Rocky Mountain air would numb his pain.

While lying on the chaise, he slowly sipped the coffee and watched as the sun rose, as if to steal the last bit of darkness Adam was able to take comfort in.

"Good morning, Adam. Do you mind if I join you?"

Startled, Adam looked around to see who he thought was Libby. He blinked and realized Sarah was standing in the doorway holding on to a cup of coffee. Adam smiled.

"Hey, Sarah. Good morning. Yeah, of course."

"Thanks. So I see you couldn't sleep either."

Sarah smiled a guilty smile at Adam, like they were partners in crime, a crime of not being able to sleep. Adam sat up and returned the sheepish smile.

"Unfortunately, not. It was tough being in Libby's room. Everything about that room breathes fresh memories with her. Then, seeing her wedding dress, that was tough. So, I came out here just to take in the Rocky Mountain air. To get some quiet time, you know?"

Sarah picked up a couple of throw blankets, dropped one in Adam's lap and then went to the chaise next to his and sat. Adam splayed the blanket around his bare feet. She wrapped herself in her blanket and proceeded to sip her coffee. For a few minutes, both of them sat in silence. Sarah spoke first.

"Yeah, I understand. I love the stillness of sitting here watching the sun rise, listening as everything in the mountains start to awake, usually anyway. These last few mornings, it feels like I am only imagining the sun is actually rising, imagining that any breathing thing is waking up and stirring to greet the day, as I am."

Adam looked at Sarah, and he could see she would never be the same. The glisten in her eye, the singsong melody of her voice, were gone. Adam realized he had done this to her and wondered if she would ever be able to get over it. Tears welled up in his eyes.

"I know what this question is going to sound like, but, how are you, Sarah? Are you going to be all right?"

Sarah closed her eyes for a moment and took a deep breath before turning to look at Adam. She noticed he looked helpless and broken. She smiled at him as best she could. She could feel it was a weary smile, one of sadness.

"I feel as if I have slipped into some sort of alternate universe, Adam. It is like there is a glass separating me from that time and the one existing for me right now. I can see that life plain as day. Libby, I can see her next to me. I can hear her voice in the house, as if she is in the other room. I can feel the anticipation and expectation that she will be there when I look up. Instead, I am here, trapped behind this glass, looking into a time that once was. This is absolute torture. I want to go back to the way things were, but it is like I am missing the key, or the password, to allow me to go back to the life I loved. So, instead, I sit here trying to make sense of this new life I am forced to live. I feel lonely. I feel empty. I feel as if we are the ones who died, and rather than being in heaven, we are living in this place, a place my mind remembers, because I can't let go. It's as if Liberty is still alive and out there, somewhere, living, going on with her life, happily."

Sarah paused for a moment.

"Adam, I feel like I merely exist in the eye of my mind and all of *this*, time and place—and suffering, is something I have made up to help me stay grounded."

Adam realized most people would have said something like, "I'm fine," or "No, I'm not okay, but I'll get there," or something short, direct and to the point. Liberty's family was not like most people. They talked to one another, really talked.

"I am just so thankful for Karl, you know? He helps keep me anchored. He is so angry about the situation, but he still knows how to stay here, focused, with me. This is a tough time for both of us, you know."

"Yeah, it's a tough time for us all."

Sarah quickly caught how self-absorbed she sounded and looked at Adam.

"Of course, darlin', I'm sorry; how are you holding up? Are *you* going to be all right?"

"I'm devastated. In the past, when we have all come together, it's been to celebrate a milestone or a success. The worst part is we are here, in her childhood home, and she is not. I never thought this would be an occasion I'd have to bear when it came to Libbs. She was the sun that made everything bright. I can't imagine a world without her in it. Libby truly deserved a long, happy life, you know? She was such a giver."

Both of them took a deep breath and turned to watch as the sun lit up the sky. Neither said a word for the rest of the sunrise. They allowed the hot tears to roll down their cold cheeks.

41

"ADAM, I'M GOING TO THE CREEK to practice some yoga. Interested?"

"Sure."

For the next hour, Adam and Sarah embraced the moment with sun salutations, warrior, triangle and other poses. When it was over, they placed their hands at their hearts in prayer pose and bowed forward toward each other.

"Namaste."

"Namaste. Thank you, Sarah; that is what I needed."

"Anytime. Pancakes?"

Adam chuckled. "Thanks, but no, not now anyway. If you don't mind, I'd like to see where Lib, uh, I'd like to go find Libby in the tree grove. Rain check?"

Sarah nodded, saying nothing in return. Instead, she put her palms together as if in prayer, brought them up to her heart and smiled before turning away to return to the house.

Adam proceeded to the tree grove and stopped when he got to Libby's tree, the Thinking Log. The spirit of Libby was there. He could smell it in the air surrounding this little piece of paradise or, as Libby would say, her little "slice of life." He could feel her as the breeze lightly blew past him, tousling his hair. He could hear her in the leaves and the grasses as they swayed with the breeze. In his mind, he could hear her laugh and hear her voice calling to him:

"Adam . . ."

He looked up at the Thinking Log, and from this vantage point, he could see the sky through the swaying leaves. It was cool. He could also see the pegs Libby had fastened into the trunk to help make her climb that much easier. Slowly, Adam placed the palm of his hand on the trunk of the tree and closed his eyes, in submission, as if to become one with the tree in order to humbly, albeit gracefully, ask, and receive, permission to climb her. When he felt the approval, he placed a foot on the first peg and reached up so the strength of his hand would pull him upward, using a higher peg as leverage. Each step was on a sturdy wood piece cut twenty inches long and screwed into the tree, which was sanded smooth and weatherproofed. Each of the pegs had a cutout on the top so fingers could make a grip. It appeared it had been a while since it was last weatherproofed. Adam presumed that making the pegs had been part of a home-school arts and crafts assignment. Karl had probably helped her carve out the cutouts. Adam continued climbing.

He noticed a peg engraved with the words "never stop loving." He paused for a moment to take in the message before looking up to confirm the remaining distance. Seeing that he was close, he continued his climb until he made it to the spot Liberty claimed as her own. When he got there, he saw Libby had refined her tree space with climbing rope, securely tethered to the trunk of the tree, to allow for ease of climbing up and back down again. Adam was unsure how she had fallen; each peg felt secure.

He looked out and was humbled by the beauty surrounding him. He could see all of the northern part of her family plot, the house, the creek and barn. In the distance, he could see the full erection of the San Juan Mountain Range. It was beyond beautiful. The branches of this oak tree were strong and grew perfectly to allow a person to sit securely as if lounging on a chaise, so he made himself comfortable. He had been here once before, with Libby, but it was during a moment in time that would be life altering. He hadn't embraced the moment for what it was. This time, however, Adam took it all in. This time, he noticed all of Liberty's niche places making this thinking place unique, and that was when he noticed a small ditty sack. It was attached to the tree arm, wrapped with a hemp tether and secured with a bead-decorated slipknot. The design was quite intricate, probably learned in another home-school arts and crafts project. He relaxed the tether, pulled the bag toward him and noticed there was a bit of Mary Jane neatly rolled into cigarettes, secured in a waterproof ziplock baggie.

"Ha! Well, I'll be damned."

He wondered how long this had been here. He unzipped the baggie, pulled out a cigarette and placed it beneath his nose. It smelled potent. He looked at the contents of the bag and noticed a lighter. He pulled it out and smiled.

"Fucking Liberty and your 420 moments."

He leaned back with the cigarette and looked out. At this moment, Adam saw life as Liberty had seen it, as if she were sitting there with him, showing him the way. Mesmerized by the beauty, he began to reflect on his own life and what had become of him.

WHEN ADAM HAD FIRST NOTICED LIBBY, like, really noticed her, it was at a bar. He and his friend Al had gone to the end-of-semester bash, and he was hoping to hook up with a Colorado hippie chick, one last time, before moving back to California. He went to the bar to get a drink and noticed Libby sitting there trying to avoid the cowboy who was trying to hit on her. What he noticed was, for the first time in his knowing her, she was wearing makeup, and she had done something creative with her hair, braiding a small section and pinning it back. That one little thing made her already beautiful face really stand out. Al noticed her first.

"Damn, is that Liberty?"

"Yeah, it is. I'm going to go talk to her. See you later." With that, Adam approached Liberty. He sat there for a few minutes attempting to gauge if she was interested in the cowboy talking with her. He heard most of the conversation and realized Libby was not interested and decided to interject.

"Is this your drink?"

When Liberty looked at Adam, she gave him a big smile and then quickly appeared to be disinterested. It was cute and he thought she would be fun to hook up with. Liberty was a closet nerd. She got top grades but was never one to mention it. While she loved being noticed for her brilliance, she hated labels, titles, or any sort of unsubtle public attention, unless it came from her parents. Their affection, their opinion, was what drove her to succeed, and was all that mattered to her. What others thought of her was of no concern. Either you liked her or you did not. If someone did not like her, she would shrug it off but would still treat them nicely. Her kindness to rude people pissed Adam off.

For Liberty, it was all about how you treated others, and strangely, how you treated yourself. She had this weird mind-set that if a person could not see the value in him (or her) self, then how would they be able to recognize the value in others? On the flip side, how could a person expect someone else to recognize their unique qualities if they were unable to be kind to someone who was unlike themselves?

She was of the opinion that people who pinned their titles, awards or what Libby called "labels" to their chests were shallow, pretentious fuckers and couldn't be trusted. Libby once explained it was because labels on lapels allowed people to hide behind a false sense of power or security, allowing them to feel entitled to something more than someone who did not wear their label, or some bullshit like that.

It was frustrating to Adam that she didn't get pissed off at people for treating her rudely, especially when she had been so nice. He wished just once he could have heard her say, "Fuck you, you fucking fuck." He believed he would have respected her more. He would have laughed his ass off, for sure, but it would have been out of respect. Instead, he had to listen to her kumbaya ideals of "Can't we all just get along?"

These liberal, home-school, hippie ideals disgusted him, and he blamed her parents for how clueless Liberty was about life in the real world. People were not as nice and kind as she believed them to be. Liberty trusted everyone and believed she needed to take care of the downtrodden few.

Adam recalled the times he yelled at her had been when she did the stupidest things. One winter, she gave away an expensive tweed coat to a homeless-looking woman because she was walking in what Libby described as "see-through pink pajamas and slippers while pushing a grocery cart down the street." The coat had been a gift to Libby. Liberty explained she didn't need things; that people and love were what a person needed for true happiness.

It wasn't that she liked giving to people in need that bothered Adam; as a matter of fact, they both tried to give when possible. It was the fact that she walked with this "homeless" woman to a boarded-up apartment building where, inside, there were mounds of boxes of clothing that had been given to her from local charities. The woman was trying to tell Libby she didn't need her coat. Libby left it with the woman anyway, explaining she couldn't take it back.

"Wait, you walked with her to a boarded-up apartment building?"

"Yes! I wanted to see how she was surviving. I needed to be sure she wasn't living in squalor."

"Weren't you afraid?"

"Afraid of what, Adam? She is just a person."

"All right, so what did you see?"

"She had a lot of cats, she had heat and running water, but her house was dirty. She appeared to be a hoarder. There were boxes of clothes given to her from charities that were stacked one upon another, up to the ceiling. They filled up her bedroom. I'm not sure how she was able to sleep with all of that stuff around her."

"So, why didn't you just take your coat and leave?"

"Adam, I couldn't just take it back! What kind of person would that make me? First, I give; then I take back because — because what, Adam?"

"How about because she didn't want your coat? How about for the fact she was trying to give it back to you by showing you all of those boxes of clothes?"

Libby also had a habit of picking up hitchhikers. The first two she thought were chicks, but turned out to be dudes. The first was a dirty hippie, and the second was a cross-dresser. Adam firmly stated she could have been raped or worse, murdered. Libby interjected, "Actually, Adam, being raped would be worse than being murdered."

"What? How so?"

"Well, with rape, my whole soul would be taken, and I would be walking around in an empty shell, but with murder, it would just be my life. My soul would still be free for whatever comes next, after death from this life."

She would follow that kind of mind-blowing opinion with a defense of her actions by saying something stupid like "Besides, I wasn't raped or murdered. If you give goodness to the world, it comes back to you, sevenfold."

Then she would explain if she didn't help a fellow sister, they could become victim to some random asshole truck driver who could have raped and murdered them. The last person she picked up she knew was a man. This was when Adam had yelled at her.

"What the fuck, Libby! Are you looking to get raped?"

"Whoa! Wait a minute, Adam, you asked me not to pick up another hitchhiker while driving alone. This time I was with my friend Bubba. You remember him, don't you? We were on our way to the beer festival in Denver."

Adam closed his eyes and let out a heavy sigh.

"Yes, I remember Bubba. Why in the hell would he let you pull over?"

"Let me, Adam? Besides, he sat in the back seat so he could strong-arm the dude if anything happened, but nothing did."

"But, Liberty, seriously, were you worried a truck driver was going to pick him up?"

"No, silly, it was windy and I could see a storm coming in. This man was so skinny, I thought he was going to blow onto the road and someone's car, like mine, was going to hit him. So, I decided to help him get to a safe place before the storm hit. On the drive down, he shared that he recently learned his sister was diagnosed with cancer and he needed to get home to Philadelphia. Instead of just dropping him off at a random spot in Denver to continue his hitch, I bought him a one-way bus ticket to Philly and a good lunch. I also gave him, like, fifty bucks to get him by for a while. Between you and me, I think he had just been released from prison and didn't have anywhere to go but home. I mean, at least that is what I gathered from the shoes he was wearing."

"*What?* Fuck! Liberty, do you read the signs saying do not pick up hitchhikers, prison nearby? This man could have raped *and* killed you. Then what would you have?"

The last two statements were made in an attempt to muddle Liberty's idealist logic. Adam wanted her to see that people were not all good.

"This guy wasn't going to rape *or* kill me, Adam. He was just a lonely soul trying to make his way to a place that felt like home. I just helped a brother out, that's all. If more people would help a fellow sister or brother out, the world would be a much better place. Besides, what if you, or I, were in that same situation?"

"Damn it, Liberty, first of all, neither one of us would be in that situation. Secondly and finally, stop picking up hitchhikers, period! Seriously, I need you to stop being so fucking nice to people. Pleeaase."

Even as Adam recalled these stories, he became irritated. This was the kind of shit Mandi would never do. She would have passed those people by without a second thought because, for Mandi, it was all about personal responsibility and accountability. If a person wasn't willing to help themselves, then why would they want her help? Why should she feel compelled to help them?

As he sat there contemplating all that came with loving Liberty, he realized this overly kind personality was what had pushed him away. Yet, on the other hand, it was exactly what had brought him back to her. Liberty never judged anyone, especially when it came to him. Adam lit his cigarette, took a few tokes and inhaled deeply.

As Adam exhaled, he felt a breeze blow by. It was a nice feeling, cleansing. Adam closed his eyes, leaned his head back into the tree and took in everything around him. He could hear the wind as it moved through the valley, the birds as they called out to one another. He realized he was like a branch of this beautiful tree, a small part of this enormous world we live in. At that moment, he heard movement below. He looked down and saw a small herd of deer. He watched as each deer made its way slowly through the grove and as it walked away.

"So fucking rad— "

ADAM CONTINUED TO ENJOY his own 420 moment, all the while thinking about his life with Liberty. At this moment, he realized he and Libby had never really discussed losing the baby. He hadn't known how to bring it up. What was he going to say? "Hey, I followed you to the different clinics. I know what happened."

All that morning, Libby had been wandering from room to room, as if looking for something she had misplaced. When Adam tried talking with her, she would look at him with distant eyes. It was evident that her mind was focused on something else.

"Hey Libbs, what's going on?"

"Nothing."

Nothing, that is what she said without looking at Adam.

"Hmm, okay. So what's your plan for the day?"

She walked past him without answering.

"Libby!"

"What, Adam? What? Nothing is wrong! I'm not doing anything! What do you want from me?"

"I just want to know what's going on. Are you all right?"

"Yes, I'm fine. I'm just thinking."

"Thinking about what?"

"Nothing, Adam."

"I see. Well, let's go for a hike today."

"I can't. I'm driving to Denver to do some shopping, you know?"

"Yeah. Denver. You hate shopping."

"Well, I don't hate it today. Look, I just need some time to myself, okay? See you later."

And that was how Adam knew something was wrong. Libby talked about her problems. That day was different, so he decided to follow her to Denver, and was how he discovered what she was so torn up about.When he realized that she had picked a clinic, he waited.

His plan had been to approach her as she was exiting the clinic. His thought had been to invite her to lunch so they could talk about the subject maturely, and potentially discuss ending the relationship. He had purchased a bouquet of fresh cut ranunculus and was holding them when she walked out. The plan was to present them to her as a peace offering, of sorts. That look, though, as the door opened and he saw her, changed everything. As she was leaving, he began to stand, but he stayed seated when he saw her face, ashen white. Her eyes, hollow, vacant, soulless. It was startling. She didn't see him seated in the lobby waiting for her; instead, she walked out, wrapping her sweater tightly around her chest, her gaze fixed upon the worn carpet path to the door.

Leaving the flowers on the empty chair next to his, he stood and followed her out as she walked to her car. He watched as she clenched her hands tightly around the wheel and then tucked her head between them, crying. She sat there, in this position, for quite a while. What he should have done was console her, but he didn't know how. Instead he went to his car and pulled it near the parking lot exit so he could follow her home, to make sure she made it back safely. He felt guilty for not knowing how to be there with her.

After that day, he chose not to continue the relationship with Mandi. His new plan was to make sure Libby pulled herself out of this funk. He started with the small stuff, by bringing her fruit plates with vitamins and continuously checking in on her. She kept trying to push him away, but he didn't let her. After all, he was the reason she was in this funk. The least he could do was be there for her, even if it was after the fact. Eventually, he called Sarah and explained he was worried about Libby.

"Hey, Sarah, it's me. Got a few minutes to talk about Liberty?"

"Adam?"

"Yes, it's me. Is this a good time?"

"Sure, darlin', of course. Is Liberty all right?"

"Yeah, I suppose. She just hasn't been herself since, um, you know—since she lost the baby. I haven't seen her smile in a while."

"Hmm, yes, I've noticed. She's more curt when she calls, and she's in a hurry to cut the call short when I ask about it. Karl has noticed it, too. We've both been concerned."

"Well, I was thinking maybe Libby and I should move in together next semester. We could get a two bedroom or something; just until the girl we both know and love is back. What do you say?"

There was silence on the phone for a few moments.

"Hmm, that is a big ask. Is that what Liberty wants?"

"Well, we haven't talked about it, yet. I wanted to talk with you and Karl before talking with Liberty, you know, since the last time didn't go so well."

"Yeah. That was not a good time. Hmm, let me talk with Karl. One of us will get back to you."

At the end of it all, Adam admitted to himself that he truly loved her, yet he had always tried to push her away, though he did not understand why. It was not that she was overbearing. She was funny, witty and could see light in everything. Libby was happy, free in her heart and her mind. Actually, Libby was pretty fucking hot.

Kissing her was magical. When their lips touched, it was as if Cupid's arrow sprinkled fairy love dust right as they kissed—a magical potion. Whatever it was, there had truly been a chemistry in their kiss. Her breath became his; his breath became hers. The flow, the unity of their kiss, that was what tripped Adam up most when it came to Liberty. He would yearn for the chemistry of that kiss.

When she was with Adam, she put all of her focus on him and made him feel significant, important, as though nothing else mattered. Libby had this way of making home a mellow place where she would dim the lamps and brighten the rooms with fragrant candles. She wasn't big into TV, but would keep herself entertained with a glass of vino and a book, or chats with him resting his head on her lap. She would caress his head with gentle temple massages or running her fingers through his hair. They would talk about nothing and everything. Libby truly made him feel loved. He had never felt like that with anyone else, not even Mandi. He felt relaxed around her. Even here, Libby's spirit managed to make him feel relaxed and at home.

Thinking about her now, the one image that repeated itself in his mind was of her, walking in front of him, at Coronado Beach. It was one of those lazy days when the best thing to do was to sit at the beach on loungers, under an umbrella, with a cooler of snacks and drinks. They were flying kites that day, and Libby was a few steps ahead of him. She turned back to look at him, and the chocolate ribbons of her hair fanned out, blocking the sun so he could see her face. She was smiling that radiant smile of hers and cheerfully calling out to him.

"Adam, come on. Catch up to me."

Then she blinked, laughed and turned around.

The image was like a freeze-frame snapshot in time. He could hear the ocean sway, the sea gulls chatter, the sounds from other people absorbing the energy from the sun and families enjoying their time at the beach. Even here, sitting on the Thinking Log, he could feel the energy of that day. It never went away when he replayed that moment. Even now, a thousand miles away from the ocean, deep in the heart of the Rocky Mountains, he could hear the sweet sounds of the Pacific, like melodious chimes blowing in the wind. Even with Libby gone, he could hear her voice, feel her energy, surrounding him.

Adam finished the remainder of the cigarette comprised of nature's remedy. He tucked the lighter back into the bag, and noticed a feather. He also noticed strips of paper with notes scrawled on them. He pulled them out and read them, one at a time. The notes were like mantras, thoughts, written down as if to release them. They read:

"He blew my mind wide open."

"Liberty Rose Anderson, mother (in spirit) to Samsara Jade."

"Love

is like the blood in your veins,
is like the air we breathe
it is sustenance."

"Everybody—

is crying in the rain.

Everybody—

is screaming with the trains now.

Everybody—

is waiting to see me smile, with the sun and the
moon as it climbs the sky.

But as the world it turns and turns and turns,

as the world it turns and yearns and earns, now,
as the world it turns and earns and burns—
(Except me)
I'll get over you."

Adam sighed, placed the notes back into their rightful places and made sure the bag was sealed tightly and tethered securely. It was evident the mantras were written at different times, based on the scrawl fluctuations. Even as much as he loved her, it was clear their relationship had become stale a long time ago. He should have let the relationship fizzle out after the loss of their baby, but the guilt had kept him around.

He closed his eyes for a few moments, and he could hear the magic of the mountains. The trickling creek, the rustling leaves, the sound of the breeze blowing by. It was mellow, beautiful and calming, like nature's medicine for the soul.

It was said when a person's soul was called to the mountains, it was looking to heal. Rather than resist, one should go to the mountains and let nature calm the soul, so it can heal properly. You should stay until the healing is completed. If you leave too soon, you might never heal. Adam breathed in nature's medicine and hoped for a miracle.

44

SARAH RETURNED TO THE HOUSE along the stepping-stone pathway she and Karl had created with Liberty. As she reflected, she recalled her life in San Francisco and just how different it was from Colorado. She and Karl had participated in life around their community by attending the rallies and protests when required and writing about them in underground newspapers. Her biggest accomplishment with Karl was when they helped a minority community in "The Mission" get federal funding for a medical facility, and then worked with the community as it was built and established. As an independent, educated woman, she'd had a voice, and she had used it.

She had loved her life in the city with Karl and had been excited about what it could become. They had hiked and camped at Big Sur, Yosemite and as much of the north coast of California and Oregon as possible. Her favorite trip, however, was after they were married. For their honeymoon, they traveled to Morocco, to Andalusia and finally to Damascus, to Lebanon and to parts of Israel.

When they returned to San Francisco, they discussed a life plan to include children; the plan was to have two. After a year, they made the leap to move to Colorado and start their family. Being pregnant with Liberty was the most joyous occasion, the little kicks while she was in the belly, her birth, rocking her to sleep. Sarah's parents came out to visit often, which was very helpful in the early years. They had both passed away nearly fifteen years ago.

Getting pregnant a second time, well, that just didn't happen. Sarah wasn't as devastated as she thought she might be and loved Liberty with all of her heart. She worked to give her the best life of independence and freedom any young woman could hope for. To teach her all she knew.

At the stepping-stone walkway, she paused to embrace the memory each step brought. Each stone reminded her that as much as she had loved San Francisco, the peace that came from this private refuge was more than she had ever imagined feeling. *This* is where her heart was.

Each stepping-stone was different, except for two similarities. The first similarity in each rock was the shaved mica they had added to the surface of every stone. The mica would give off a sparkle at night, like bread crumbs to allow them to find their way back home after their stargazing strolls. As part of her English classes, Liberty had been reading fairy tales from the Brothers Grimm. One of her favorites had been "Hansel and Gretel," specifically the concept of leaving bread crumbs, or secret clues, behind so the children could find their way home. She also liked the idea of leaving bread crumbs so people who loved you could find you, if needed.

The second similarity was each stone provided a memory of Liberty. Each represented a time when they had all worked to create their little pathway masterpiece, with handprints, paw prints, birth dates, hearts and fun-shaped rocks. Sarah smoothed over each intricate detail. Where there were handprints, she placed her hand over the cast as if to relive that moment. With each step, a different memory of Liberty flashed through her mind.

She finally made it home and, to commemorate the memory of her daughter, started to whip up Liberty's favorite, smashed banana pancakes stuffed with blueberries and walnuts. The house was quiet. Sarah assumed everyone was still asleep. It was only seven in the morning. A few moments later, Karl came into the kitchen. He stopped to kiss Sarah lightly on her neck and then poured himself a cup of coffee.

"Morning, sunshine."

"Hey, baby. How'd you sleep?"

"Ehh. I suppose okay. You were up early. Yoga?"

"Mmm, yeah. I heard Adam this morning. He didn't sound well. That was around five. He came down to make coffee. After a while, I decided to join him for a cup and a moment of solitude. After the sun rose, we both went to the creek for yoga."

"Ah. So, where is he now?"

"The Thinking Log. He went to find Libby in the grove."

"Hmm, isn't that a little profound? It takes her death for Adam to search for Liberty. Do you think he really ever knew her?"

"Karl."

Karl chuckled a little, brewed a fresh pot of coffee and pulled out ingredients to make egg scrambles. He and Sarah started to prepare breakfast, just as they would on a normal day. A few moments later, Peter and Mazy entered the house. Peter came to where Karl and Sarah were standing. Mazy pulled out two cups and poured coffee for herself and her husband. Peter spoke.

"Hey, good morning. You two look better than yesterday. Did you sleep well?"

Karl and Sarah looked at each other and then at Peter. Both said, "Eh."

"It's getting a bit easier, now that Adam and his family are here, but once they leave, I am sure it will be trying, once again. Adam had a difficult time sleeping last night and got out of bed at five this morning. I came down and watched the sun rise with him and then practiced yoga by the creek. Yoga was much needed."

"Hmm, sounds like a nice morning. Where is Adam now?"

"Mazy, Adam finally made an attempt to find Libby in the grove."

"Maybe this is what Adam is needing, to heal," Mazy said. "You know, a semblance of what Libby was last doing. Everyone is hurting. Imagine what he is going through. He and Libby were planning to be married. This cannot be easy. I don't know what I would have done had I lost Petey before we married."

"God bless your mother; she tried to break us apart, darlin'. One of these days we are going to have to forgive her. It's been twenty-five years."

"Maybe, Petey."

At that moment, silence took over, and the food was prepared for their still-sleeping guests, and Adam. As they were finishing up, Diane came downstairs.

"Hi. Good morning. Sorry I slept so late."

"No, please, not at all, it's early. Did we wake you? Would you like some coffee?"

As soon as Sarah made the offer, she was pouring Diane a cup.

"Mmm, thanks, Sarah. No, you didn't wake me. I finally fell asleep when Adam stopped crying and woke up when Richard started to snore. I am heartbroken for Adam. Poor guy, I think he is still asleep."

"Yeah, I heard Adam all night as well. He got out of bed around five this morning. He is actually at the Thinking Log, where Libby, um—"

"He's looking for Liberty."

Karl didn't know why he had to be so abrupt about it. He knew he sounded like an asshole but could not help it.

45

SITTING ON THE THINKING LOG, experiencing what Liberty had experienced so many times before, Adam finally understood his lost love at that deeper level. In her way, she had found freedom in her heart and mind, and in that instant, he finally realized why Liberty was so kind. Life in this slice of paradise was a rarity. Not everyone could have moments like these all of the time, if ever. Libby had experienced this tranquility every day from the time she was a child. As if opening his eyes for the first time, Adam was instantly humbled by the beauty of nature this vantage point, this Anderson family refuge, had to offer. He felt as if he had experienced being born again, in the spiritual sense, after breathing in the life embodying Mother Earth.

In that moment, Adam remembered Mandi and thought of how she must have been pissed. He quickly reached into his pocket to send her a text message and remembered he had left his phone broken in pieces across her patio; the same way he left Liberty on the beach after telling her he had AIDS. Libby had been left with a broken spirit within that beautiful body of hers.

What was it in Mandi that compelled him to want to leave Liberty? Why had he felt the need to lie to her about the AIDS virus? He didn't have it. Liberty sure as hell didn't have it. Why couldn't he just tell her he had changed his mind and wanted out? He had convinced himself the truth would have killed her radiant spirit. He would have broken his promise not to fuck her over. He never imagined it would be his lie that would actually kill Liberty, physically. Why in the hell had she panicked? Liberty was usually more level headed.

When Adam had decided to tell the tale, he had imagined she would freak out a little bit, but would instantly get herself checked out and realize she was fine. Adam had thought if he were out of the picture, she would have the chance to meet someone, someone better than he would ever be for her. He never imagined it would come to this, the death of Liberty.

When Mandi had called him, she had offered the sense of a different life, a more fun-filled life of glitz and glamour filled with crazy parties. He had been conflicted about what he had, and what he thought he wanted, in a relationship. He told himself he was tired of Liberty's hippie homebody ways. He convinced himself they had been two different people from the very beginning. Adam wanted the energy Liberty radiated with a simple smile, but he wanted the lifestyle Mandi offered. He had hoped Liberty would grow into somebody more worldly once she stepped away from her Anderson family refuge, out of Colorado. He had hoped her exposure to other pools of life would make her want to swim in the shallow side for a while. He hoped she could be more superficial, that she would like fast luxury cars, expensive clothes and great parties. Instead, Liberty's flower-child personality stuck with her. It wasn't that she didn't find this other way of life fun; it was just not one she chose to absorb as her own.

What he had been looking for all of these years was Mandi, or someone like her. Liberty had just happened to accept him when he was discouraged in his search, and she had always been willing to take him back. He accepted Liberty's grace, even though he held it against her when she shared that same graceful spirit with others less deserving. He held other things against her, as well. For one, he had always resented her for getting pregnant and ruining what he could have had with Mandi. The only reason he ended it with Mandi was the baby.

So, when Mandi called, and after that first lunch, the feelings from before rekindled. He fell in love with her all over again. After more lunches, dinners and other trysts, he decided he would try to make it work with Mandi, especially considering there were no finalized marriage plans to prevent him from moving on. Mandi placed so much pressure on him to end the relationship with Liberty. What she didn't understand was how difficult it would be. Despite Adam's wanting his relationship with Mandi, Liberty was his best friend. To end the relationship would be more than simply saying, "It's over." They had so many years together. They had formed an emotional connection, one that couldn't be broken easily.

Adam didn't know how to just tell Libby the truth, about Mandi, and was why he had lied. He had no idea the fucking AIDS-virus lie would actually kill his best friend.

He sat in the Thinking Log, numb with sadness. Thankfully, the tree limbs were large enough to hold him in place, because the strength required to hold himself up was gone. It helped that Libby had taken old backpack straps and had created a security belt, so to speak. She had sewn holes large enough to host climbing rope. She had wrapped and tied the climbing rope around two parts of the tree so the backpack straps could adjust to fit the frame of anyone sitting there. The backpack straps maintained the original release pull system so the straps could be tightened or released as necessary, to be secured on the body, tethering the person to the tree.

During the course of the morning, Adam felt he had aged ten years. He could feel his eyes losing their sparkle, his smile disappearing and the skin of his face becoming droopy. He could feel the change. There was no way he wanted to move, but he could tell by the sun it was close to noon. The others would be looking for him soon if he did not get going, so he made an effort to descend. He remembered he was barefoot and his shoes were on the front porch from the night before. The Andersons had requested everyone remove their shoes before entering their home. They felt this would keep the bad juju out of their peaceful abode. Of all the Anderson habits, Adam was able to dig this one, and it was a custom he practiced as well, except he did it to keep sand and dirt off of the floors.

As he was descending, he could feel every peg and noticed one peg was not as secure as it should have been. When he was at eye level with it, he assessed and noticed it was loose enough to shift if weight were applied.

"Hmm, is that what happened? Did Libby lose her footing on this peg?"

He wanted to mark it, but didn't have anything with him. So he counted the pegs on his way down, with the loose peg as peg number one.

"I'll need to fix this before I leave, or at least tell Karl about it."

Once Adam was down, he proceeded toward the house, onto the stepping-stones and up to the patio door. As he entered, he noticed everyone was eating brunch.

"Hey. Sorry I took so long out there. I was at the Thinking Log."

"You're not late. We all went back to bed and slept in. We just sat for breakfast. Grab a plate, and sit with us. The food is on the table," Sarah said.

"Yeah, sure. Thanks."

"So, did you find Liberty?"

Karl could be contemptuous, at times, Adam thought. He closed his eyes in disbelief. The last thing he wanted to deal with was Karl. He finished washing his hands, dried them and took a plate. When he turned around, he gave a half smile and responded.

"The Thinking Log is an awesome hideaway. I can see why Libby liked going there. If you don't mind, I'd like to go back. I noticed one of the pegs is loose. I'll fix it if you show me where to find the tools."

Adam's voice was hollow. His voice startled everyone at the table, and all heads turned toward him. They could see he was suffering, and everyone proceeded to eat the remainder of their brunch quietly. Karl watched Adam for a few moments, trying to read him. Sarah reached her hand to Karl's knee and squeezed it gently. Karl took a bite of his eggs and watched as Adam filled his plate.

"Loose, huh? Hmm. Yeah, I'll go with you."

46

AFTER BRUNCH, ADAM EXCUSED HIMSELF and went up to Liberty's room. It was the most comfortable place in the house, like a cocoon. He lay back on the bed, closed his eyes and placed his hands over them while rubbing his forehead. His head was aching and he was exhausted. Thoughts of soaking in a hot bath came to mind, and he sat up slowly as a first effort to move toward the bathroom. However, once he entered, he looked in the mirror and realized he might fall asleep if he took a bath, so he opted for a hot shower instead.

The pressure from the hot water spray seemed to wash away a few layers of pretense Adam had hidden behind his entire life, exposing the kind of man he had allowed himself to become, at the core. He felt raw. After the shower, he returned to Libby's room, and tucked himself deep under the covers. He was exhausted. It had been a fucked up twenty-four hours. He closed his eyes, told himself he would need to call Mandi, as she must be freaking, and fell asleep. He slept most of the day, but no one seemed to mind. Everyone else was busy preparing for the actual commemoration services, for Liberty, that would be taking place the next day.

Peter and Rich spent the day gathering chairs from the barn storage room, wiping them clean and moving them to the plot. Neither said much, but both were glad the mountain weather seemed to be working in their favor. Mazy and Diane drove into town with the directions to purchase ribbon and various fabrics to make seat covers for the chairs. They stopped at the local coffee shop to grab a coffee to go. It was nice to be away from the house for a while, Diane thought, and she opted to slowly peruse.

Sarah and Karl climbed up to the Thinking Log to write Liberty's eulogy.

"Be careful, Sarah. Adam said one of the pegs is loose. He didn't mark it, so I'm not sure which one it is."

"Okay. Did you bring something to fix it?"

"Yeah, I have a few tools in my pocket. Feel for each peg as you go up and let me know if you find it."

"All right."

Karl found the peg himself, and his immediate urge was to yank the damn thing off the tree. Instead, he placed his hand over the peg, and tears welled up in his eyes. Sarah noticed he had stopped climbing and looked down.

"Everything okay, Karl?"

"Uh, yeah, I found the peg. The screw has somehow loosened."

Sarah leaned her forehead against the tree trunk, taking her own pause from the moment. Karl pulled out his screwdriver and began to tighten the screw. Once the peg was secure, he took a piece of sandpaper to clear the weatherproofing varnish. Then, he pulled out a small spray bottle of liquid dye he had made, using crushed flowers and other samplings of nature's hidden treasures, to mark this little thing that made such a huge impact on his life—on the life of his family. Once that moment was marked, even embraced, Sarah and Karl made their way to Libby's spot.

"Karl, do you remember when Libby first learned to climb this tree? I was so nervous watching her, but so proud when she accomplished her feat."

"Hmm, yes. Do you remember when she said the Thinking Log needed to be better? I remember offering to help her build an actual tree house. She looked at me and said, 'Dad, why would I want walls to block out all of that?' Then she stretched out her hand and waved it as if to point to everything she could see. She made me a proud papa that day. My mother would have been elated."

"Your parents would have adored her."

"Funny, I was thinking about them today. I really miss them, even my dad's 'rules.'"

"Darlin', you are the man you are because of his rules, and I am grateful, because I would have you no other way."

"Thank you, Sarah. I love you, too."

"Can you believe we lost both our only child and our grandchild in one day?"

"Second grandchild, Sarah. Let's not forget about the first one."

"Mmmm. Do you think Adam knows Libby was pregnant?"

"Hmm, good question. Let me ask him, Sarah. Don't mention it, okay?"

"Okay."

They stopped talking and looked out while sitting in silence, searching for the perfect message to memorialize Liberty.

47

THE SUN WAS STARTING TO SET. Adam had been awake for almost an hour, but he continued to lie in bed while gazing out the window. He watched as the light changed colors and as the shapes of the shadows took on a new form. He didn't want to get out of bed. He didn't want to talk about the reality of this visit. The house was surprisingly quiet.

He decided to get up and be a part of the "milestone" for which everyone had gathered. He sat up and pulled his legs over as if to get out of bed. He noticed again Liberty's wedding dress hanging on the closet door, and took a long breath. He threw on a long-sleeved shirt, a pair of jeans, and decided he needed to brush his teeth, hair and anything to make him feel like he had his shit together.

Before leaving the room, he stopped to put his hand on the dress. His finger moved gently across the intricate details, taking in every nuance he thought Libby might have included as her signature. Adam could see her wearing the dress. She would have been beautiful. He smiled at the thought of seeing her and stepped away to clean himself up. Once he was satisfied with the way he looked, he went downstairs to be a part of the family.

"Hey, how's it going? I can't believe I slept the day away. Sarah, do you mind if I make some coffee?"

"Hey, Adam, no, not at all. *Mi casa es su casa.*"

Adam chuckled and proceeded to make the coffee.

"Thanks. So what did you all do while I slept?"

Karl was making drinks for Rich and himself. Rich was sitting on the sofa next to the fireplace. Everyone noticed Adam seemed to be feeling better. Rich spoke up.

"Well, Son, while you caught up on your beauty sleep, we spent the day catching some rays, outside. Your mother drove into town with Mazy to get some decorations. They should be pulling up any minute. Peter and I spent the day in the barn cleaning chairs. Karl and Sarah were taking care of some personal stuff."

"Yeah, Sarah and I went up to the Thinking Log," Karl said.

Adam looked at Karl.

"Yeah?"

"Yeah. I found the loose peg and fixed it. Turns out, one of the screws had become loosened."

Adam and Karl looked at each other and, for the first time, shared a bit of camaraderie. Adam turned to pour himself a cup of coffee and went over to Karl, placing his hand on his shoulder.

"I'm really sorry, man. Truly."

Karl took his glass and clinked it against Adam's coffee cup and swallowed his drink whole. As Karl proceeded to pour another drink, Adam moved to his father and sat down next to him. Adam put his hand on his father's leg, and his father placed his hand on top of Adam's. They looked at each other, smiled and nodded.

Just then, Mazy and Diane came into the house with bags of ribbon and fabric. Adam placed his cup on the table and jumped up to help. Peter came in behind them with takeout boxes of Chinese food from the only Chinese restaurant in town. For the rest of the night, everyone sat around the table to eat and, afterward, to sew together ribbon bows and seat covers. Karl made sure everyone had a drink. Sarah spoke about favorite memories of Liberty, and everyone took pleasure in sharing their own favorite moments with Liberty. Some of the memories were corny, while others were sentimental and funny. Regardless, everyone who mattered to Liberty was together in her "slice of life." They pulled together, shared tears and laughter, and that was how the third day went down.

THE NEXT MORNING MARKED the big day. Everyone woke up early to make sure they were ready for whatever the day would bring. Sarah, as usual, started the day with yoga. Karl and Adam joined in. Diane surprised everyone by making breakfast and fresh coffee. Once breakfast was finished, and the kitchen cleaned, they all went to the family plot. They set up the chairs and adorned them with the seat covers and ribbon bows made the night before. Mazy added mini bouquets of flowers, using sprigs of lavender, pale pink ranunculus, eucalyptus and red poppies as garnishment to the bows. They were perfectly and naturally beautiful. Sarah slid her hand around Mazy's waist, then leaned her head on Mazy's shoulder.

"You are so wonderful, Mazy. It is really beautiful. Thank you."

Mazy didn't say anything. Instead, she placed her hand on Sarah's and squeezed it. They stood there embracing the moment, both with tears in their eyes. Eventually, the embalmer brought Liberty home. He asked his team of people to carefully take her to her final resting place, where Karl and Adam led them. They carried her carefully, finally placing Libby's casket gently into the area Pete and Karl had carved out for this moment. Once this was completed, the men gave their condolences and left. Everyone took turns placing a shovelful of dirt over the casket. Karl and Adam finished the deed.

Once that was finished, they sat a couple of seats away from one another and stared at the site. Everyone else had gone into the house to freshen up for the guests who would soon be arriving for the actual end-of-life celebration. After a few moments, Karl turned to Adam. Adam felt Karl looking at him, but ignored the look. He really did not want to answer any of Karl's questions.

"So, Adam, how are you doing?"

Adam continued looking forward and down.

"I'm all right, Karl, considering. You?"

"Honestly, Adam, I'm a bit perplexed about all of this. I don't understand why Liberty came home. Did you know she called in to work saying she had a family emergency to attend to here in Colorado?"

Adam turned to look at Karl, and started to play with his fingers, nervously.

"No. I wasn't aware." Adam continued to look at Karl, wondering where he was going with this question.

"Yeah, and then I found this business card in her rental car. It was on the floorboard. I figured it fell out of her bag or something."

Karl reached out to hand the card to Adam. Adam took the card and began to read the front.

"Check out the back."

Adam turned the card over, and instantly his stomach churned. He thought he was going to be sick. He stared at the card.

"Do you know what the fuck that is about? Was Liberty sick?"

Adam shook his head, not knowing what to say.

"No. Uh, no she wasn't. Not that I was aware of anyway. She didn't say."

"Hmm, so that's the part I am most perplexed about."

Adam looked at Karl. "Yeah, how so?"

"Well, because Liberty told you everything. I would think you would be the first to know if anything were wrong with her."

Adam closed his eyes, then looked out to the site, and then to the flowers.

"The other perplexing piece of this is you didn't even know Liberty was here in Colorado. And then you asked if Liberty had committed suicide. What are you not telling me, Adam?"

Adam stood and slowly began to pace. While trying to figure out what to say, he ran his fingers through his hair. Karl immediately felt an "oh shit" moment coming and wasn't sure he would be able to handle it. He continued to stay seated as Adam rambled. Each word spilled out slowly. Adam wanted to be as truthful as possible, to clear his conscience.

"Well, Karl, I, um, I don't know how to tell you this. Liberty and I were having some issues. I moved out a couple of days before she came out to visit you, which is why I didn't know she was here. I assume her emergency was about that."

Adam turned to look at Karl, as if gauging Karl's sensibilities.

"Issues? You moved out? Liberty didn't say anything to us about your having issues, which is odd, because she tells us everything."

"I moved out because I felt I had betrayed Libby and thought she could do better than me. You see, this girl from my past showed up one day. As you know, Libby and I had a rocky road. In between our breakups, I dated other women. Well, one of those women told me she had the AIDS virus, told me I probably had it and that I should get tested. Libby was pissed, as you can imagine. We had an argument and I moved out. That was the last I had seen or talked to Libby."

Adam realized he couldn't tell the whole truth.

"So, then, the test results must be about that, eh, Adam?"

"Yeah, I would say so."

"So, do you have the AIDS virus?"

"No. My tests were clean. I would imagine Libby's will be, too."

"Did you ever tell Libby you were clean?"

"No. I thought she would figure it out herself and then hate me for the rest of her life. I figured she would be better off without me."

Karl sat there in disbelief, thinking, "Who in the hell is this guy?" Adam sat down and placed the doctor's card in the chair next to Karl's. He put his head in his hands. He knew Karl was livid, and he was waiting for Karl to punch him. Karl looked at Adam several times trying to spit out some words, but couldn't. Finally, he spoke. His voice was hoarse.

"So, yesterday, I called the number on that card and spoke with Dr. Whiteman. Nice lady. She told me Libby had visited her office the day before coming out to Colorado, distraught, because her fiancé told her he had tested positive for AIDS. That fiancé would be you, right, Adam?"

Adam did not respond. He stood, turned his back to Karl and began to pace. Tears fell down his cheeks.

"Dr. Whiteman also said Libby explained she would be coming home, to Colorado, to tell us about the situation as she waited for the results, so we could all work through this ridiculous notion together. Would you like to know what her results were?"

"They were negative."

"Hmm, of course you would say that, right? Because you lied to Libby, convinced her you had AIDS, moved out leaving her in a frenetic state. Well, the results came back positive."

Adam jolted around to face Karl. His blood seemed to dissipate through every pore and crevice. He thought he might faint. He sat down. He opened his eyes wide in his ashen-white face and replayed the last sentence, "The results came back positive."

"Wait!" Adam paused to comprehend what had just been said before continuing, "Wait. What? Libby tested positive for AIDS? There has to be a mistake, a false positive or something! Maybe the results got mixed up!"

Karl watched Adam's freak attack, and became somewhat amused by it. He leaned back and let Adam experience what Libby must have experienced when Adam gave that same news to her.

"Well, shit! Is that how she died? Did she kill herself by allowing herself to fall out of the tree? Who could have given her AIDS? She said she had only slept with two other people in her life. Did she leave a note?"

Adam was panicking, his mind reeling as he tried to figure out the who and the how. Karl was no longer amused. Instead, he was becoming more angry.

"Wait, I could have AIDS! That bitch!"

"You motherfucker," Karl said. "Libby didn't test positive for AIDS. Why would she have? Her pregnancy test came back positive. Liberty was pregnant. Did you know that?"

"Pregnant? What? Wait, pregnant? Oh my God! Fuck!"

Adam leaned back in his chair, firming his feet solidly on the ground to hold him up. His hands went up to his head, then down his face. He covered his mouth, all the while staring out to deal with the reality before him. He closed his eyes and began to cry.

Karl picked up the card and went to the house. Adam sat there alone for a while longer, tears streaming down his cheeks.

49

SLOWLY, A LITTLE BEFORE NOON, people began to arrive. Friends from the local community brought amazing home-cooked delectables from their gardens. There was plenty for everyone to share in after the ceremony. Families of the children Libby had been home-schooled with came. Libby's close friends showed up, as well as a few people Libby had worked with. Adam spent most of his time with Libby's friends and colleagues while Karl and Sarah comingled with their neighborhood pals.

When it was time, Mazy used the music triangle to bring everyone to attention. The ping sound was like a sonar echo ready to pull everyone into the full life of Liberty, an independent, liberated young woman. An echo to remind everyone just why they were all here, in this place, at this time.

"Hello, everyone. For those of you who do not know me, my name is Mazy Upchurch. On behalf of the Anderson family, we would like to extend a humble *thank-you* to each of you for joining us as we welcome our sweet Liberty Rose back to her childhood home. My husband, Peter, and I have placed flowers in the two baskets you will see on either side of this path. Please take a stem, and kindly follow us to Libby's new home."

Sarah reached out to Adam, taking his hand, asking him to walk with the family. Rich and Diane were up front waiting for him to join them. As hosts, Sarah and Karl led their friends, family and neighbors down the path, through the tree grove and out to the family plot, as if guiding the Liberty tribe to a place of peace. The walk led them past the path markers, made by Liberty, which led to the creek, where Libby would play alone or practice yoga as well as stargaze with her parents, and finally to the tree grove, past the Thinking Log, where Liberty would spend her free time contemplating life, all it meant, to herself and to others. Where she spent the last of her waking moments contemplating everything leading to this point in her life. The tribe of Liberty quietly, gently walked past the place where her soul was set free.

Finally, they crossed the field where, as a family, they used to picnic and watch the clouds roll by, and they went on toward Libby's final resting place. Everyone stopped talking and followed, one by one, along the trail. It was a beautiful day. The sun was shining. The trickle of the creek was calming. The birds sang melodies that mellowed the moment. When they arrived at Liberty's place, everyone sat down, except for Karl and Sarah. They stood facing their loved ones while holding each other's hands. Karl spoke first.

"Thank you all for coming. As you can imagine, and will probably attest, Liberty's passing was unexpected. Sarah and I were unsure how many people would be able to make it, especially here, to our home in the middle of God's beautiful country, which isn't easy to reach. For some of you, there was flying time, which included the waiting time to transfer from whichever airport you flew into, just to be here to celebrate the end of a life we were all lucky to be a part of, and to say a final good-bye to Liberty Rose. For that, Sarah and I thank you. Please know we are truly humbled.

"Liberty was our only child. Sarah and I gladly gave up our careers, our life in the city, to make sure Liberty had the best quality of life we could provide her, one of innocence and lessons inspired by nature's goodness. It is here that Liberty grew up. If you look around, you will see what she would term 'a slice of her life' before some of you knew her.

"One of her favorite places was what she dubbed, 'the Thinking Log.' It started out as a small tree Libby was able to climb. Every day, her mother, Sarah, would send her out to do some exploring and to come back with a story. Of course, one or sometimes both of us would follow to make sure she didn't get hurt, but inevitably she would always go to this little tree, her 'Thinking Log.' Over time, as she grew older, so did the tree, and the tree grew taller. She made that place up there her very own. Libby continued to climb that tree every day she was here. It was her place of refuge, I suppose. A place she went to 'think' about things."

"It's funny," Sarah chimed in. "When Libby would return each day, she would run in with excitement reciting a story she had made up. The story would always begin with 'I went to the Thinking Log today, and you won't believe what I saw.' Karl and I took great pleasure in her stories. That is where Liberty was during this visit. I imagine she would have returned home saying, 'I went to the Thinking Log today, and you won't believe what I saw.'"

Sarah laughed nervously, and everyone laughed with her. Karl squeezed Sarah's hand gently, brought it to his lips and kissed it. Sarah looked up at him, smiled and leaned into his arm for a moment. As Adam watched, he realized how wrong he had been about Sarah and Karl. They really did love each other. Their kind of love was indeed possible. The way they looked at each other was with genuine care. Adam looked at his parents and smiled. He knew his parents loved each other, but they didn't love each other in the same way. Karl spoke again.

"Yes, Libby came home this time and went straight to her private hideaway. We weren't home when she arrived. We learned her whereabouts with a note she left informing us the car in the driveway was hers, and she was at the 'Thinking Log.' It has been determined, as she was climbing down, one of the pegs she would use for grip and leverage was loose. We suppose it shifted when Libby stepped on it, which caused her to lose her grip, slip and fall thirty feet. Our doctors have said she died instantly and didn't feel any pain.

"Unfortunately, that is how we lost our daughter, your friend, and why we are all here today; to release Liberty with love and to celebrate her kindness and generosity. That said, we shouldn't give all of our attention to how she died, only. Sarah and I think we can each say something amazing about how she lived her life as she had the most beautiful spirit of anyone I know. She loved, truly loved, everyone she met. Even if she was not fond of a person, out of love she would be kind. Always generous and, unfortunately, would sometimes let the wrong person into her life. Although she would never see it like that."

Everyone chuckled as if they agreed. Karl shot a look at Adam. Adam knew Karl meant he was the wrong person she had let into her life. Adam agreed.

"As you all know, Libby was engaged to be married to Adam. Sarah and I thought we would give him the honor of closing out the family eulogy by saying a few words. Adam?"

Adam was taken aback. In his mind, the only word he could come up with was, simply, "Fuck." His mother patted his knee, and both his parents smiled at him, offering a bit of encouragement. Sarah went to him and grabbed his hand to lead him to the front. She reached up to kiss his cheek and stepped away, smiling. Nervously, sheepishly, Adam faced everyone who was there. He paused to look at every single person in front of him. He looked down and began talking, using words he thought sounded like gibberish, the only language he felt he was qualified to speak at this point.

"Hey. I'm Adam, Liberty's fiancé. Um, as Karl mentioned, this event was unexpected, and I'm not sure what I should say. So, I guess I'll start with how we met and go from there. I promise I'll try not to bore you all."

Everyone chuckled, including Adam.

"Before I do, if you do not know Mr. and Mrs. Anderson well, let me tell you they are pretty amazing parents. They raised an outstanding young woman who died too early, unnecessarily. They are also pretty amazing people. If it were not for this horrific circumstance for which we are gathered today, I am not sure I would ever have understood just how amazing they are: this place, the way they raised Liberty, the way they have welcomed my family and me with open arms, all of it. Karl, Sarah, thank you for this opportunity to speak.

"So, Libby and I met in Fort Collins, where we were both going to college. For the longest time, I tried to figure out, 'Why me?' Of all of the guys out there, why did Liberty fall for someone like me? She was so much smarter than I, such a better person than I could ever be. Eventually, I chalked it up to chemistry. There was something between us that just drew us together, like magnets."

Adam looked up again, and at the back row, he saw what seemed to be an image of Libby. She was in her wedding dress. An image of what he imagined she would look like if she were really wearing it. He felt his mind was playing tricks on him. He choked up a bit, and tears began to stream down his face. He blinked a few times, wiped his eyes and continued. The rest of what he said was directed to her.

"When I first met Liberty, I thought she was beautiful, witty, free spirited and kind, so kind. When she smiled, it made my world seem complete, as if I were the only one she allowed to see 'that' smile. I fell in love with her immediately. We quickly became friends, best friends, and started to explore what life had to offer as much as we could. All of my adult memories, to this moment, have Liberty in them, and if I could change any of them, it would be only to have more memories of Liberty. When I arrived this week, I went up to the 'Thinking Log,' and for the first time, I had the opportunity to see this slice of life as Libby saw it. It's beautiful. It's free. It showed me how lucky I was to know her as well as I did. It showed me how I would like to have known her better. Liberty Rose Anderson, you are the most beautiful person I will ever have the pleasure of knowing. I loved you from the moment we met. I love you now. I will never stop loving you."

Adam began to walk toward Libby's apparition. The image led him to the tree grove, to her tree, and he fell to his knees repeating the words, "I'm sorry, Libbs. I am so sorry. Please forgive me."

After a few moments, Karl and Sarah realized Adam would not be returning. In an effort to pull the attention away from his emotional breakdown and back to Liberty, they asked if anyone else would like to say a few words.

"Thanks, Adam," Karl said. "As you can imagine, this is not an easy time for any of us. Adam is especially having a hard time losing his fiancé. At this time, we would like to open this celebration of Liberty to all of you. Liberty was selective with her friends. It would be nice to hear your experiences with her, so that we may get to live vicariously through your stories."

Many took the opportunity to share their favorite Liberty moment. Karl and Sarah reveled in the love others felt for their daughter. Karl felt for Adam; he did. He knew Adam was suffering, but Karl was not ready to console him. He was angry. Rich and Diane subtly walked away from the service to find Adam. When they did, he was on his knees at the foot of the Thinking Log, repeating apologies to Liberty. Together, Rich and Diane helped him up and walked him back into the house.

"Hey, Son, are you all right? Would you like to talk about it?"

Rich was deeply concerned, as was Diane.

"Yeah, Dad, I'm all right. This is just such a fucked-up situation here. Did you know Liberty was pregnant?"

Rich and Diane were taken aback. They looked at each other, then at Adam. They held on to his arm. Together, they said, "Oh, Son! No, we didn't know."

"Yeah, I found out this morning. Karl told me."

"That's tragic," said Diane.

"If you don't mind, I'd really like to be alone."

"Yeah, of course. Your mother and I are here when you are ready to talk."

Adam stopped to give his father a hug and his mother a kiss on the cheek.

"Thanks, you have no idea how much that means to me. I love you. I love you, both."

Adam turned and went upstairs to Libby's room where he changed into more comfortable clothes. Then he left and returned to the Thinking Log. That was where he felt closest to Libby and was where he wanted to be.

He enjoyed another 420 moment, and stayed there until everyone had left. He stayed until the sun finished its final descent beyond the horizon.

"Libby, why in the hell didn't you tell me you were pregnant?"

Adam asked the question out loud, knowing it would never be answered. He considered what the child might have been, male or female. He imagined Libby as a mother. In his mind, he formed pictures of moments that would never occur, of Libby pregnant, holding the newborn baby for the first time, bringing him or her home; Libby's smile and her grace as she would teach the child how to live, Liberty-style. He created memories of a time that would never take place, of family camping trips, sailing trips, memories of the three of them growing together, as a family.

Once the sky had blackened, Adam slowly made his way down the tree and back to the house. He stopped at the creek and splashed fresh cold water onto his face. He did that three times before walking on toward the house. He stopped on the patio and looked inside through the glass. Sarah and Diane were sitting on the sofa, sipping glasses of wine in front of the fireplace. Karl and Rich were nowhere to be seen, and Adam wondered where they might be. He imagined Mazy and Peter were back at their place. He suddenly started to feel cold.

"So, Adam, are you going in or staying out here?"

Adam jumped. He turned to the voice and saw it was Karl who had spoken. Karl was lying on the chaise, covered with a blanket, waiting for Adam. It was dark and hard to see. Karl chuckled.

"Grab a blanket and a seat if you want."

"Where's my old man?"

"He went for a drive, said he needed some air."

"Oh."

"He mentioned you told him about the baby. Did you tell him anything else?"

"No, just that Libby was pregnant. Does Sarah know?"

"Not yet. I'll tell her when I think she can handle it."

Adam took a blanket and sat on the chaise next to Karl. Neither man said a word. The only sounds were those of the mountains at night. It was still. It was beautiful. It was home.

After a while, Karl sat up and folded his blanket. He looked at Adam and said his last few words to him.

"Look, Adam, I don't know the whole story between you and Liberty and this mess that appeared to cause her death. You should just know I think you are a real son of a bitch for the way I think you might have handled the whole scenario. It's the same way you handled all of the other times you wanted to walk away from the relationship. Libby never told me, but I have always been able to read what she refused to say. I'm sure you'll be leaving with your parents tomorrow. Because I know how much Liberty loved you, I am going to say I wish you the very best, but you should know I think you can go fuck yourself. I'm going inside now and up to my room. I suspect I shan't see you again. So, with that, good night. And take care, Adam."

Karl went into the house, explained to the ladies just how tired he was after this long day and how tomorrow would be an early day for him as there was plenty of cleanup to be done. He wanted to go to bed. The ladies bid him good night.

Adam replayed the words Karl had recited. He had said them so calmly. Each word was like a dagger sliding smoothly into Adam's skin, through to his heart. It was a stab deep inside where the cut would itch, but could never be scratched. Where the wound would never heal. Adam reached his hand to his chest; there was no blood. This was the second time today that Karl had cut him with the sword of his words. Karl was smart like that, so that he could knock you on your ass without lifting a finger. After Karl had gone up the stairs, and Adam felt like he could breathe again, he proceeded to fold his own blanket and went into the house. Sarah and Diane were happy to see him, as they had been worried.

"Heeeyyy! Come sit with us."

"Sure. Do you mind if I have a glass of that?"

Adam pointed to the half-consumed bottle of wine. Sarah nodded. Adam selected a glass from the bar and poured. He folded into the sofa in front of the fire, not saying a word. Sarah and Diane were talking to each other in whispered tones about how Sarah and Karl had discovered the news about the pregnancy. Both spoke of "what if" scenarios. Ultimately, their words sounded like buzzing bumblebees, and he quickly tuned them out. Instead, Adam stared into the soft burning flames in the fireplace, tuning in to the thoughts of his mind.

In the way that shadows can cast images, the softness of the flames turned into a memory of a beautiful Pacific coast day. He and Liberty were at the beach. He was able to hear Liberty's melodic voice as she called out to him. He could hear the sounds of the sea gulls and the flow of the ocean waves as they moved onto the shore and retreated back into themselves. Mostly, he could see the brown ribbons of Liberty's hair dance, as she bounced before him, blocking the sun's rays, which allowed him to see her beautiful face and her radiant smile. He could hear her laughter, and her voice as she called out, "Adam, come to me."

Adam absorbed the heat of this memory as it played over and over again in his mind, like a loop. Tears graced his hot cheeks. To him, this image was real. Rich finally returned, and eventually, everyone went to bed. Adam didn't notice. He stared ahead at the images lit up by the flames and stayed there until the fire burned cold, like a starless night. The image faded and Adam was left sitting alone, in the dark with the thought of how insolent he had been, not only to Liberty, but to Karl and Sarah. Karl was right to be angry with him, but at this point, there was nothing that could be undone: the tears, the broken hearts, the lie, her death. Nothing would bring back the joy that once consumed this house like a fire on the mountain. He would live with this for the rest of his life, all the while searching for redemption, for ways to make amends for the biggest wrong of his entire life.

The house was quiet, except for the soft hum of the electronics. His smile vanished. He finished his glass of wine and then looked down at the empty glass. His fingers traced the rim, down the side of the glass to the stem and then down to the base. This was his life. Fully consumed, empty. Tomorrow would be a new day, the beginning of a new life, and he seriously did not want to go back to that place without her, without his family. He took in a deep breath, then closed his eyes. The silence was comforting.

Tomorrow would be a new day, a new life, and he would have to force himself to endure it as there would be no going back to yesterday. If he could, he would go back to November, when Mandi first called. He would have met her for lunch, and he would have told her about his engagement with Liberty. He would have kept his promise to her. Mandi would have moved on to someone else, and Adam and Liberty would have continued planning for a wedding, their wedding. They would be learning about a child they would be bringing into this world together, and there would be a moment, like this weekend, where everyone gathered together to raise a champagne flute to toast the beauty of a new dawn, a new day. To celebrate *life*!

Adam realized he would not be able to return to Mandi. Not now. How would he be able to live with himself? Every touch of her skin would singe and radiate deep as a constant reminder that his deception had caused the demise of his greatest love. Rather than return to California tomorrow, he would take his backpack and get lost in the wilderness for the remainder of his time away from work, to take in nature's remedy. The heart of the mountains beckoned him.

"Adam. Come to me."

a note from the author

THANK YOU FOR PURCHASING and reading *The Thinking Log*. The idea of this novel was sparked from a rumor I heard at a funeral. The rumor being the deceased had committed suicide after learning his wife was diagnosed with AIDS. The controversy of the rumor was the wife had told the deceased he had AIDS as well, but she wanted to end the relationship rather than deal with it together. According to the story, the deceased learned more about AIDS and didn't want to die with the "shame" of having it. He never got himself tested. In truth, she didn't have AIDS. Instead, she had fallen in love with another man and wanted a divorce, but used AIDS as the reason to end her marriage. The story of this horrid lie broke my heart for the deceased and his family. I helplessly watched as his mother suffered with deep anguish. I wondered how one person could be so callous to another once called husband, best friend and great love. Because of that event, the concept of *consequence* became more real to me, especially with other people involved.

That was almost thirty years ago, when news about AIDS started to circulate in rural, small-town America, when very few people understood what it really meant to have this disease. As my friend Barry described it, and as we should all know, a lot of people have "fucking died" from this disease, "the plague of our generation." Families, and lovers, have had to live with the stigma, and were treated in the most vile way, which is why the rumor about this great lie bothered me so much. I just couldn't fathom the rationale behind the insolent wife. The idea another person can so willfully kill the soul of a living person, in this way, makes me angry! Even still.

From that moment, I have sought a way to tell this story without implicating anyone related to that story. *The Thinking Log* is my attempt. The characters and the story are fiction. Remember, the idea of this story comes from a *rumor* I heard at a funeral.

That said, HIV/AIDS is not fiction! It is a real disease that affects real people, like you and me, and people we may know. Take a moment to learn the latest stats, which can be found on www.HIV.gov, or at your local HIV/AIDS support center. If you do not know where your local support group is, type in your city name in the service locator search box on that website. *Get tested!* If your test result is positive, please try to remain calm and find a support team to help you get through this uncertain time. If you know someone who may be dealing with this disease, *please*, be kind. Show them love and compassion. No judgment.

To give back, 30 percent of the purchase price of this book will go to charitable causes like AIDS organizations that help to medicate, and potentially eradicate, the disease, as well as to agencies geared to protect and preserve this great land and ocean that I love.

Personally, I like to lose myself on a trail with a backpack loaded with whatever I need to survive, as there is something about climbing a rugged path to a summit point that leads me to self-realization, clarity, purpose and peace. It is what I did when I was younger, and where I believe I discovered the answers to my many questions, where I discovered just who, and what, I could become when "lost in the wilderness" or during moments of quiet contemplation while watching the sun set over the ocean. I want my nieces and nephews, and generations after them, to be able to explore the wild beauty of Mother Earth and to find the meaning of life in the backcountry, and deep ocean waters, just as I had the privilege to.

Hopefully you share the same passion about eradicating a terrible disease and preserving the great outdoors as I do. If so, then together, we *will* make a difference.

Again, thank you for reading *The Thinking Log*.

With love, peace.
Rachel

giving thanks

THE ONE CONSISTENT LESSON I've learned throughout my adult life is that no amount of progress is made alone. For me, a dreamer, it's my family and close friends who listen to my ideas and help me stay on point or listen to my woes only to give me amazing words of encouragement to keep me moving forward. These fine folks make up my foundation, my grounding.

And then there are the unexpected folks, the silent helpers, the ones who have held enough of a modicum of confidence in me to want to help open doors without my realizing it, until the doors have been opened. It's humbling. It is these beautiful beings who make me want to become a better person, so they feel glad about their choice to help me. After all, they could have chosen to help someone else.

Writing *The Thinking Log*, and self-publishing the novel with It's About Love, has proven to be the same type of experience. I have worked with really amazing people to get this through to the finish line. And let me tell you, it's been my most fun experience of 2017. Along with gaining knowledge about the process of self-publishing a book, I have also had the privilege of meeting really amazing people, like Sally Arteseros and Katie Herman, my rockstar editors, as well as, Tamara Dever and Erin Stark, book designers with TLC Graphics, Chris Stewart, Paul Williamson and Joe Hinton, my attorneys, and Aubrey Cypert, the lady who helps manage my funds. I would also like to thank the team of people at the Writers League of Texas for answering my endless questions, as well as JJ Huckin, for his mad camera skills. Without even knowing me well, and sans hesitation, this team of beautiful people has given the best advice, corrected my grammatical and formatting errors and introduced me to folks within the industry, with the sole intent of making *The Thinking Log* a book you would want to read, and I am grateful.

And then, there were my writer friends, Donna Flenniken, Barry Cochran, Thom Smith, and close friends and family. These beautiful creatives took time away from their projects to read my novel and give me pointers on what was missing, what could be better and what should be eliminated.

I have also had the opportunity to call on people from my past: Tony Freeman and the Cenveo team, who printed *The Thinking Log*, and Alexa McDonald and Justin Smith, two amazing designers who have taken my ideas for my logo and website design and made them better, and Djiipu, who spent many a weekend making a beautiful music piece for the book trailer.

Lastly, there's you, the reader. Thank you the most for deciding to spend your hard-earned money to buy *The Thinking Log*. The money you spent will not be used in vain. Thirty percent will be given to charities to help strengthen the fabric of our society, and ensure that our community is sound for the people of tomorrow. Together, we can do something great in this world, because no amount of progress is made alone.

I hope you enjoyed the book.